HILL'S HEROES VOLUME 1

Malcolm Snook

Cover Picture Andrew Carnegie. The man who started it all.

INTRODUCTION

In the course of reading Think And Grow Rich you will have found that Napoleon Hill drops in all sorts of names and stories to illustrate his points. In some cases he mentions partnerships such as 'The Moore Boys' or the 'Wright Brothers' but give or take one or two there are some 150 names mentioned.

Where the illustrations are particularly important, key stories or turning points in the lives of these people are told to us, however, it should be remembered that in many cases Napoleon Hill was writing about people who were household names in his own day. In quite a few cases those names are well known to us now, but their life stories are not so well known. Most people know the name Ford, they see it every day in most countries, but the younger generation may not know the founders name was Henry or why his automobile company was so successful when others have come and gone.

Some of the people mentioned are naturally of great significance and others merely a passing reference of small moment. However this three volume book will supply you with some brief details you may wish to know about each of Hill's Heroes, and there's a spreadsheet as part of the package for quick easy reference to the most basic facts and in many cases links to third party websites where you can discover more, or related interesting material should you wish to take the time.

You will find the length and detail given in the following biographies varies. I have decided how detailed to make each one based on three factors, how much is already told to us in Hill's own book, how much of the information I believe is of particular relevance, help and interest to those wishing to know more about Hill's philosophy and how much the person concerned has impacted our lives today. Of course much of this is subjective and a matter of personal opinion and I take full responsibility for my choices in going into greater detail in certain instances.

Should you choose any of these people as your imaginary counselors then indeed you should study their biographies in detail and try to understand their attitudes, philosophies, strategies and decision making processes.

So, starting with Napoleon Hill himself prepare to meet the cast of Think And Grow Rich.

1.   Napoleon Hill

Napoleon Hill was born October 26th 1883 to James and Sarah Hill. His mother died when Napoleon was a ten year old lad running wild and undisciplined around the vicinity of the one room cabin the family lived in, on the Pound River in the beautiful Appalachian Mountains of Wise County Virginia. It is claimed the young boy was even carrying a pistol at that tender age.

When Napoleon was twelve his father married again and Napoleon's stepmother Martha transformed the lad. She also inspired his father at the age of forty to take training and become a qualified dentist, until then he'd been practising illegally without formal qualifications. Napoleon's father died in 1939. Whether the story that Martha persuaded Napoleon to swop his pistol for a typewriter is true or not, he himself certainly acknowledged her influence. He graduated from High School in 1900 but from the age of thirteen had already been writing for local journals.

Just as Napoleon Hill's early life was one of trials and harsh lessons, so his later life involved many tribulations and setbacks, he was not immune to depression or melancholy either, but always bounced back, a true measure of character and a testament to the wisdom to be found in his writings. He tried to pay his own and his brother's way through law school from his journalistic earnings as a young man. He experienced a failure in that goal which must have been heartbreaking as both he and his brother had to drop out of education.

At one stage Dr. Hill founded a magazine, but was later pushed out by his own employees. Another business partnership also faltered. The lessons he learned are there in his writings for all of us to see and profit by. Two divorces, the second of which cost him his fortune from his first successful book and other tribulations such as the drying up of royalties in the depression and the birth of a profoundly deaf son mark this remarkable life.

And yet, not only is Napoleon Hill remembered as one of the great philosophical and motivational writers of his age, he also worked for no less than two American Presidents and found time to teach advertising at the La Salle Extension University. He was on the PR staff of Pres. Woodrow Wilson during World War I and a presidential advisor to Pres. Franklin D Roosevelt. He helped his son overcome his disability through never allowing him to acknowledge any disadvantage, a lesson we can all profit from.

In 1908 Napoleon Hill interviewed steel magnate Andrew Carnegie for a magazine article. If the introduction of his stepmother's influence was a seminal moment in the creation of Napoleon Hill's character, the interview with Andrew Carnegie was the turning point that laid the foundation for his monetary success and his ability to recover from each and every setback. His book Think And Grow Rich effectively tells the rest.

In later years Napoleon Hill experienced financial stability and a happy marriage to a good woman. His journey led to ultimate success and development of character, it's a journey we can all learn from. The decency of the mature man, who may once have covered up another's crime in his youth, shine through in many of his quotes, two of which are reproduced below as illustrations.

Quotes:

"Before us lie two paths – honesty and dishonesty. The shortsighted embark on the dishonest path; the wise on the honest. For the wise know the truth; in helping others we help ourselves; and in hurting others we hurt ourselves. Character overshadows money, and trust rises above fame. Honesty is still the best policy."

"War grows out of the desire of the individual to gain advantage at the expense of his fellow man."

2.   Dr. Miller Reese Hutchinson

Born August 6th 1876 Died February 16th 1944 Born and raised in Montrose Alabama, across the bay from Mobile Dr. Miller Reese Hutchinson is best known for the invention of the Acousticon hearing aid; in fact he was also responsible for the Dictograph, the Klaxon horn and an early eavesdropping device amongst over 1000 patents.

He graduated from Auburn in electrical engineering, which was at the time a very young subject. He served in the Spanish American war before going east and pursuing a career which led to his becoming chief engineer to the world renowned inventor Thomas A. Edison for a time, and to a meeting with Queen Alexandra of Great Britain in 1902.

He also played an important role in promoting the use of the Edison Storage Battery in US submarines of the period.

3.   Thomas Alva Edison

Born Milan Ohio February 11th 1847 - Died October 18th 1931.
The youngest of seven children Thomas Edison received only
a few months of formal education. The family relocated to
Port Huron Michigan when the lad was seven and at thirteen
he was selling newspapers and candy. Not the most
auspicious start for the man who would become the greatest
inventor of his generation, arguably of the twentieth century.
However, his mother had taught him reading, writing and
mathematics and he was an avid, self motivated reader of
science and technology.

By sixteen he was a proficient telegrapher (telegraph operator)
and worked in various cities before arriving in Boston in 1868
where he began his career as an inventor with a patented
electric vote counter, it proved a commercial failure. However,
in 1869 he moved to New York, married Mary Stilwell, started
a family and invented his 'Universal Stock Printer' a ticker
tape machine that netted him $40,000 and enabled him to set
up a laboratory and manufacturing facility in Newark, New
Jersey. (It's amazing the impact of one man on America and
the world, from music, light, power and movies to ticker tape
parades!)

In 1876 he set up a new laboratory some twenty five miles south west of New York at Menlo Park. Here he invented the tin foil phonograph, the forerunner of the vinyl record player and an invention that brought him international recognition. His next invention and possibly the one that changed the world the most was the incandescent light bulb, after, by his own admission thousands of failed attempts. He used this new invention to light his own laboratory and almost single handedly created the electric power industry, which of course led to thousands of electric devices for use in the home. The company later known as General Electric was originally Edison General Electric, but although a major stockholder Edison had insufficient capital of his own to control the company and following a merger his name was dropped from the title.

In 1884 Mary died and in 1886 Edison married Mina Miller and moved to West Orange, New Jersey where he built another new laboratory, at its peak in World War One it would cover twenty acres and employ ten thousand workers. Edison sold his stock in General Electric to fund research into iron ore mining equipment, he lost a fortune, but restored it with his continuing work on the phonograph and pioneering work in the field of moving pictures.

In 1915 he was made head of the Navy Consulting Board and in 1928 he was voted a lifetime achievement medal by Congress. If all the above were not enough he also invented the alkaline battery and at the request of his friends Harvey Firestone and Henry Ford pioneered the creation of a new type of rubber for automobile tires. He was still working in the year of his death, 1931.

Quotes:

I have not failed. I've just found 10,000 ways that won't work.

I find my greatest pleasure, and so my reward, in the work that precedes what the world calls success.

If we did all the things we are capable of, we would literally astound ourselves.

I am proud of the fact that I never invented weapons to kill.

Genius is one percent inspiration and ninety-nine percent perspiration.

Being busy does not always mean real work. The object of all work is production or accomplishment and to either of these ends there must be forethought, system, planning, intelligence, and honest purpose, as well as perspiration. Seeming to do is not doing.

Anything that won't sell, I don't want to invent. Its sale is proof of utility, and utility is success.

It is astonishing what an effort it seems to be for many people to put their brains definitely and systematically to work.

I know this world is ruled by infinite intelligence. Everything that surrounds us- everything that exists - proves that there are infinite laws behind it. There can be no denying this fact. It is mathematical in its precision.

Hell, there are no rules here - we're trying to accomplish something.

Discontent is the first necessity of progress.

4. Dr John R. Turner

Dr Turner was born February 15th 1881 in Matville, Raleigh county, W Virginia and died October 7th 1969 in California. He was the son of William Turner a Captain in the Union Army who had been wounded at the battle of Cross Keys. Dr John Roscoe Turner graduated with a Ph.D. from Princeton in 1913 and later became Professor of Economics at Cornell University, Dean of Washington Square College of New York University and from December 1928 to 1934 was President of the University of West Virginia.

His published works include: The Ricardian Rent Theory In Early American Economics, Introduction to Economics and Modern Business: Economics, The Science of Business.

He married Eleanor Effie Vertner on August 23, 1905 in Ohio.

5. Blair Hill

Born 1912 son of Napoleon Hill and Florence Elizabeth Hill nee Hornor. Although born deaf he never learned sign language and was later able to hear with the aid of an electronic hearing aid, he became a successful salesman for such devices.

6.   Andrew Carnegie

Born November 25th 1835 – Died August 11th 1919 Andrew Carnegie was a self made industrialist who emigrated from Scotland (Dunfermline in Fife) to the USA at the age of thirteen with his parents William and Margaret. William was a linen weaver but also a campaigner for improvements in the conditions of the working classes – an interesting early influence. Andrew's first job was as a bobbin boy in a cotton factory, later he became a telegraph operator (note the coincidence as Thomas A. Edison had the same job for a period). In common with Edison, Carnegie was an avid reader, after a local citizen opened his private library for use by working class boys. Carnegie himself would later demonstrate his gratitude and understanding by endowing numerous schools and libraries.

He founded the Carnegie Steel Company in Pittsburgh after progressing from telegraph operator to a more senior role with a railroad and then investing in a company that made railway sleeper cars. This led on to bridges and other industrial enterprises and finally steel making. Probably as a result of his father's influence his policy was always one of treating his workers as partners of capital.

Think And Grow Rich tells the story of the creation of US Steel, and the sale to JP Morgan of Carnegie's assets. What it doesn't tell us is how Andrew Carnegie used his millions as a great philanthropist and peace campaigner, founding among many things The Carnegie Endowment For International Peace based in Washington. Note also that Henry Ford was accused of being a pacifist! Truly there is a message that comes from these great men.

Carnegie's story is indeed one of rags to riches and it's little wonder that his story inspired Napoleon Hill, given that Carnegie is credited with doing it himself, and has been described as the second richest man in history. However Hill tells us that Carnegie used a Master Mind Group and made its members rich too. This supports Hill's assertion that any plan or transaction you make should benefit ALL who are involved.

Carnegie was a prolific writer (see his Gospel of Wealth). He believed the wealthy are merely custodians of wealth under a moral obligation to improve the lot of others, he believed that to die excessively rich was to die disgraced and his good works are too many to list.

Andrew Carnegie's wealth probably peaked at $475 million which by the standards of the 2000's could be as high as $297/8 billion of that $475 million he had given away all but $30 million when he died unexpectedly. He is widely considered to have been, at the peak of his financial success, the second richest man in modern history. For the richest and a comparison of relative philanthropy, particularly the proportion given away at death see John D. Rockefeller.

7.   President William Howard Taft

Born September 15th 1857 died March 8th 1930 27th President of the United States of America. Born into an already powerful family in Cincinnati, Ohio William Howard Taft's rise was nonetheless impressive. Graduated Yale 1878, then the Cincinnati Law School 1880. He was an Ohio Superior Court Judge by 1887, Solicitor General in 1890, United States Court of Appeals judge 1891 and Governor general of the Philippines in 1900 appointed by President William McKinley.

In 1904 he was appointed Secretary of War by Theodore Roosevelt and in 1908 he became President himself. His single term is remembered for trust-busting (monopoly reform), civil service reform, a strengthened interstate commerce commission, an improved postal service and passage of the sixteenth amendment to the constitution viz ' The Congress shall have power to lay and collect taxes on incomes, from whatever source derived, without apportionment among the several states etc.'

After the presidency he was professor of law at Yale and finally Chief Justice of the USA, a job he loved greatly and held until just before his death.

8.   F.W. Woolworth

Franklin Winfield Woolworth Born 1852 – Died 1919 Born to a poor farming family in upstate New York his five and ten cent stores were inspired by a five cents clearance sale he witnessed. He borrowed from his employer to start his business and initially failed, his second attempt created a business which made him extremely wealthy in his own time and which became a household name in the USA and Great Britain.

9.   Captain Robert Dollar

Born 1844 - Died 1932 Born in Falkirk in Scotland, the young Robert Dollar was a poor emigrant who worked from the age of fourteen in a Canadian logging camp. He first taught himself French which enabled him to become the Camp accountant and by the age of twenty two he was running the camp! By 1872 he owned his own camp, but it failed. Undeterred he went on to create a huge lumber business in Michigan and California.

He purchased a steam schooner (hybrid steam and sail) to transport his own lumber and continued buying steamships, forming the Dollar Steamship Company later known as the American Presidents Line. He developed American trade with the Orient and earned himself the nickname, the Grand Old Man of the Pacific. He became fabulously wealthy and, as with many of Napoleon Hill's heroes he was a considerable philanthropist, building schools and orphanages.

10. Samuel Gompers

Born January 27th 1850 Died December 13th 1924 Born in London, Samual Gompers emigrated to New York with his family at the age of thirteen. He'd been rolling cigars for his father's business from the age of ten and in 1875 became the President of the Cigar Maker's International Union in New York.

He went on to become the first and longest serving President of the American Federation of Labor. He worked to promote organisation and collective bargaining to improve the lot of the working class, he encouraged harmony among different craft unions and championed sexual equality in the work place. During World War One he worked with the government to discourage strikes and maintain morale whilst endeavouring to ensure workers' rights were not eroded.

Various monuments have been erected in his honor and a navy ship named for him.

11. John Wanamaker

Born July 11th 1838 Died December 12th 1922 John Wanamaker's third store, built on the site of an old railway depot is known as Philadelphia's first department store. Dating to 1875 it was John Wanamaker's third store, the first dating to 1861 and the second to 1869.

John Wanamaker was more than founder of a chain of stores however, he was an active religious, and civic leader, a mason and politically active. His term as the 35th US Postmaster general was controversial but did see the introduction of the parcel post.

He has been described as the father of modern advertising, but is nonetheless accredited the following quote: 'Half the money I spend on advertising is wasted; the trouble is I don't know which half!' Wanamaker was a friend of Thomas Edison who was a pallbearer at his funeral. He was known as a caring employer after whom the masons' have dedicated a medal awarded for good works.

12.   George Eastman

Born July 12th 1854 Died March 14th 1932. The father of amateur photography was born into a poor household in Waterville, up-state New York. He dropped out of high school and supported his mother and two sisters, one of whom was disabled on his initial salary of just three dollars per week. This rose to five dollars when he was promoted from messenger boy, after creating a new policy filing system and even writing policies for the insurance company where he worked.

His next step up was when he earned the princely sum of fifteen dollars per week as a bank clerk in Rochester. However his life changed when he bought a huge, cumbersome, early wet plate camera for a holiday he planned but never took. His interest in photography led to him reading about dry plates being developed in England and he started experimenting, after work, in the family kitchen to produce his own.

Before long he had a business selling dry plates, but nearly lost everything when a faulty batch went off. Nothing daunted, after compensating his customers financially, he continued experimenting, inventing roll film on paper, launched in 1884. Photographers did not flock to use his invention and in 1888 he started producing his own cameras. The brand name Kodak was his brain child and by advertising his inventions to the masses he single-handedly brought picture taking to us all.

He was a pioneering employer giving his employees dividends to share in the profits created by their labors, later he went further giving a large portion of his stock to the workforce and introducing life insurance, disability programs and pensions. Ahead of his time in these regards he was, like so many of the men featured in Think And Grow Rich a notable philanthropist. He believed in education for the world's future and gave to varied educational institutions from technology to music and created dentistry clinics for children in cities within and outside the US.

13. William Wrigley Jr.

Born September 30th 1861 Died January 26th 1932   Arriving in Chicago from Philadelphia aged 29 William Wrigley Jr. promptly founded a company to sell Wrigley's Scouring Soap, a product manufactured by his father. He was a natural salesman and got on well with his customers. He offered his merchants free baking powder with the soap. When the baking powder became a good seller in its own right, he offered them free chewing gum as an incentive with that and before long when the chewing gum proved popular a new business empire was born!

14. Charles M. Schwab

Born February 18th 1862 Died October 18th 1939. Charles Michael Schwab was born of German Catholic stock in Pennsylvania. Napoleon Hill tells us of Schwab's being the catalyst for the founding of, and first president of US Steel, the world's largest steel company at the age of thirty nine. Unlike others amongst Napoleon Hill's heroes Charlie Schwab did not operate a harmonious master mind, nor was he a great philanthropist. He also died broke.

Having fallen out with J.P. Morgan and Elbert Gary he left US Steel and formed Bethlehem Steel. He took a huge risk (he's reputed to have told his secretary, 'if we're going bust, we'll go bust big') but pioneered the steel girders that made skyscrapers a reality in New York and around the world. Bethlehem steel becoming the second largest steel company in the world as a result. However, he was a profligate spender and built a mansion covering an entire block of New York. It was later considered too grandiose even for the mayoral residence, tragically it was later torn down and replaced by a drab tenement block.

As well as spending big he also gambled and carried on extra marital affairs. His flamboyant lifestyle and taxes on his property left him poorly placed to deal with the depression and he died in debt, living on borrowed money in London in 1939. Ironically World War Two steel orders restored the fortunes of Bethlehem Steel. Some nineteen of his heirs reputedly netted in excess of $40 million each when it was sold off in the 1980s.

15. Arthur Nash

1870 – 1927 Arthur Nash was a devout Christian and a Freemason. He wrote a book entitled The Golden Rule in Business. He took what was effectively a sweat shop and applied the maxim in relation to his workers 'If I were in your place and you were in mine, what would I want you to do?'

In 1918 the company turned over $132,000, in 1923 almost $6 million and in 1924 Nash distributed $600,000 worth of stock to his workforce.

16. Stuart Austin Weir

Born circa 1894 much of what we know about Stuart Austin Weir's life is told in Think And Grow Rich. However there are records of a Dallas lawyer which fit Hill's description; born August 21st 1894, died April 23rd 1959. He was of Irish immigrant stock although the family forbears were from Scotland. He had a son Richard Austin Weir by first wife Dunwoody or Dourwoodie Burgess. One reference shows the son as James Richard Wier, this may be an error although there were possibly twins of whom one did not survive. Another reference gives a daughter Edith Grace born 4-25-1931 by second wife Mary Price and yet another reference said Stuart Austin Wier married Mary Lindberg about 1940 around Dallas or Houston.

It seems certain that Stuart Austin Wier was a writer and lecturer as well as a Dallas lawyer. He served as an Army engineer in World War One and started a general law practice in 1931. He was also, in common with several of Hill's Heroes a writer, in this case the author of several books from 'The Art And Science Of Selling' and 'The Rise Of Individualism From A Legal Standpoint' to books on Shakespeare.

17. Jennings Randolph

March 8th 1902 – May 8th 1998 Seven times elected to Congress, Jennings Randolph was previously an educator and journalist. Following the republican landslide of 1946 which removed him from Congress he returned to academia and also accepted a PR role with Capital Airlines.

He was an aviation enthusiast and a peace campaigner; in 1946 he re-introduced a bill to create a government department of peace and in 1984 was instrumental in the actual creation of the US Institute of Peace.

18. Jesse Grant Chapline

Born July 2nd 1870 – Died July 4th 1937 Founded the distance learning facility known as La Salle Extension University and hired Napoleon Hill as Advertising Manager.

19. President Woodrow Wilson

Born December 28th 1856 – Died February 3rd 1924 28th President of the United States. Woodrow Wilson graduated from the College of New Jersey, later Princeton University. He then went on to University of Virginia Law School and finally a doctorate from John Hopkins University.

He became President of Princeton University in 1902, staying in the post until 1911 when he became Governor of New Jersey and then in 1912 became the new democratic President of the USA, the republican vote being split between Taft and Roosevelt. Amongst other legislation Wilson passed a law prohibiting child labor and was largely elected to a second term on the back of his having kept the USA out of World War One.

With Germany wooing Mexico and launching unrestricted submarine warfare against US shipping Wilson asked congress to declare war on Germany. The influx of American troops to the European continent forced the Germans into a major offensive to try and win the war before the extra numbers ranged against them could tell. The offensive failed and the end of the war was in sight.

Wilson travelled to Paris and tried to exert a moderating influence over the Versailles Treaty. He failed. He also founded the League of Nations. The Senate failed to ratify Versailles and although the League of Nations went ahead the United States failed to join. The strain led to a major stroke and although Wilson won the Nobel Peace Prize his influence was at an end and he was nursed devotedly by his second wife and survived until 1924.

The disastrous Versaille treaty paved the way for Hitler's rise and World War Two although blame for that cannot be laid at Wilson's door, nor can the failure of the League of Nations, it was the world's tragedy that his voice of reason was not heeded sufficiently at home or abroad.

20. Hon. Manuel L. Quezon

Born August 19th 1878 – Died August 1st 1944 Manuel L. Quezon is considered by Filipinos to be the second President of the Philippines succeeding Emilio Aguinaldo who was a leader in the fight, first against the Spanish and then against US annexation. Nonetheless Quezon was elected with 68% of the vote. He gave women the vote after inviting them to vote as to whether they wanted the right and he is considered to be father of the language having instigated a formal dictionary.

He was re-elected with an increased majority achieving 82% of the vote second time around. During World War Two he established a government in exile and died of Tuberculosis in New York State in 1944. He was interred in Arlington Cemetery but later his body was repatriated to his homeland on board the USS Princeton.

Quotes:

> *"My loyalty to my party ends where my loyalty to my country begins."*
>
> *"Social Justice is far more beneficial when applied as a matter of sentiment, and not of law."*

21.   Henry Ford

Born July 30th 1863 – Died April 7th 1947 Born on a farm Henry Ford did, as Napoleon Hill tells us, receive a rudimentary education. He was the eldest of six children and was frequently required to work on the family farm. He was an apprentice machinist in Detroit at sixteen, married in 1888 and ran a sawmill at that time. His interest in engineering led him to become an engineer, working for another of Hill's heroes at the Edison Illuminating Company in 1891 and chief engineer by 1893.

In his spare time Ford built his first car, the rudimentary Quadricycle as he called it, completed in 1896. Despite the name it was a car, with seating for two, four wheels obviously and a gasoline fuelled internal combustion engine. Drive to the rear wheels was by chain and it had two forward gears, but no reverse. Steering was by tiller. It wasn't the world's first automobile, but it was one of the first and Ford was truly one of the pioneers.

After two failed attempts to create his own company, the Ford Automobile Company that we know today was incorporated on June 16th 1903. Between 1908 and 1927 the company built it's famed Model T, the Model S preceded it but instead of a Model U, Ford created the Model A afterwards. Model U being a title used by a competitor at that time. Ford also stated the model A was so different it represented a new line.

The Model T, however, was the car that put America on wheels and made the company's fortune. Or rather it was the way the car was built that made the company's fortune and put America on wheels, since Ford was the father of assembly line production. This in turn achieved his goal that every working man on a reasonable salary should be able to afford one.

Although he long resisted organised labor unions Ford was good to his workers too. He introduced three shifts so his workers worked fewer hours than in other comparable companies of the era and he paid his workers a wage proportionate to the cost of the car so they could afford to own one, thereby creating his own market. It's interesting to note here that when FIAT of Italy introduced robotised production lines that would cost jobs an Italian labour leader commented to management that 'robots don't buy cars.'

By 1910 a car was coming off the Ford assembly line at the new factory, Highland Park, Michigan at the rate of one every three minutes. By 1914 the entire assembly process for each car was just ninety three minutes from start to finish. More than fifteen million Model T's were manufactured, a record not beaten until the 1970's (VW Beetle), by which time many advances had been made in manufacturing and technology and of course the world wide market for cars was much larger. Unsurprisingly the Model T was voted the most influential car of the twentieth century.

Henry Ford the man, is more difficult to fathom. Napoleon Hill tells us of a famous libel suit and he praises his hero. In fact the lawyer's approach did harm Ford's personal reputation making him appear an ill educated bumpkin. Ford won the case, but was awarded derisory damages so it might be called a draw. Attitudes may well be different in this day and age where the idea that it's more important to know where to get information than to know it yourself is perhaps more widely accepted, electronic calculators are allowed in many school exams and computer/internet use is an everyday part of life. This writer subscribes to the view that Ford was ahead of his time.

Hill makes reference to Ford's pacifist views and in World War One Ford did charter a cruise liner, loaded it with approximately one hundred and seventy high profile pacifists including himself and sailed for Europe in the hope of creating a peace conference and changing the course of world history. The venture failed, received widespread ridicule and Ford personally left the ship in Sweden. The mission had no backing from President Wilson or the US government although Ford did talk to Wilson beforehand.

One of Ford's suggestion's that received widespread ridicule was the idea he espoused that the sinking of the Lusitania was engineered by parties wishing to drag the US into the war. Germany of course acknowledged responsibility for the sinking and defended it as a legitimate act which didn't help Ford. Ironically in recent times it has been alleged that Britain's World War Two leader Winston Churchill, at that time at the Admiralty in London, deliberately withheld information about U Boat operations in the area of the attack from the Lusitania's Captain in the hope it would be sunk, and that such an action would bring the US actively into the allied fold. Despite widespread indignation in the US they did not declare war until much later (see Woodrow Wilson).

In the run up to World War Two we find mixed messages coming from Ford, he owned a paper called the Dearborn Independent from 1920 which published anti-Semitic articles. It was closed in 1927 and Henry Ford made a public apology. He disassociated himself personally from his journalists, but his apology was widely held to be insincere. It should be noted that Ford believed certain Jewish Bankers to have been instrumental in causing World War One, a position which today seems unsupportable, however, on the other side of the coin his World War One Peace Ship was the suggestion of a Jewish pacifist Rosika Schwimmer. It's at least a possibility that Ford's problem was with certain sectors of Jewish society rather than with all Jews per se.

Ford clearly believed that international trade could help in creating a lasting international peace and he built plants in many countries, including Germany, Russia and Great Britain with this in mind. His company became such a part of the British scene and such a major employer that many Briton's erroneously thought of it as a British company.

However, despite the above, Hitler was a great admirer and had a portrait of Ford in his Munich office. In 1938 Ford was awarded a Nazi medal, the highest award given to foreigners and he accepted it from the German consul in Cleveland around his seventy fifth birthday. For balance it should be noted that Ford was not alone in receiving awards from the Nazis, a GM board member was similarly 'honored' as was Charles Lindbergh. Whether Ford contributed financially to Hitler's political campaign is unclear, at least unproven as things stand, but allegations have been made.

Trucks from Ford and GM plants in Germany were used in the invasion of Poland and both companies have been accused of supplying both sides. After the fall of France, Ford himself apparently vetoed a plan to produce Rolls Royce aero engines for British fighter planes. Maybe he, like others such as the US ambassador Joe Kennedy, thought Britain's demise imminent. Once the US was at war with Germany contact between the American parent firm and it's German subsidiaries and those in occupied territories became illegal. Although Germany never technically nationalised Ford's German and French plants they were of course German managed and sadly employed slave labor. There is some debate and controversy as to whether, or how much, Ford of America benefited from this financially. After the war Ford was compensated for the damage done by allied bombing.

It's a complicated picture and hindsight does not give us a clear view. Roosevelt described Michigan as the 'arsenal of democracy' with some cause. Putting conspiracy theories and dramatist's aside it seems clear that the Ford Motor Company's contribution to allied victory greatly exceeds any contribution it may have made, deliberately or inadvertently, to the axis forces even if Henry Ford himself left most of the liaison with his own government to his son and senior managers.

We can see now, looking back, all that Hitler did, and the horrors of his regime, certainly his attitudes became more and more apparent as time went on and Ford did receive his Cross of the German Spread Eagle medal after the annexation of Austria. However this 'unification' of Germanic peoples was welcomed by a major sector of Austrian society at the time. The fact that many Jews did not flee Germany is testament that many of the appalling policies of the Nazis were not foreseen even by people living in the country, let alone those, like Ford, living on the other side of the Atlantic.

Once war became a fact Ford's contribution to ultimate allied victory was of a magnitude quite different from any contribution his factories, which tragically utilized slave labor under the Nazis, made to Germany's war machine. Forgetting all the vehicles Ford supplied consider just one example the allies' most prolific bomber, Consolidated's B24 Liberator. Consolidated could build one per day, until Ford took a hand and got production up to one per HOUR!

Ford's son Edsel sadly died of cancer in 1943 and Henry Ford himself took over the Presidency once more, by then an ailing seventy nine year old with heart problems, suspicious of his own government. In 1945 he handed over to his grandson Henry Ford II. He died in 1947 aged eighty three. His legacy remains. At its peak the Ford plant at River Rouge was the world's largest industrial complex, in 1932 Ford manufactured one third of all vehicles made in the world. Henry Ford had a lifelong passion for engineering, he registered many patents himself, produced a plastic bodied car, manufactured aeroplanes which utilised advanced alloys in their construction and won an award from the Smithsonian Institute.

His record as a pacifist was undoubtedly tarnished by his publication of the Dearborn Independent and remarks he made around the dinner table, his Nazi admirers and his acceptance of their medal. Nonetheless he was a visionary who provided mass employment and changed the face of the modern world, in the final analysis more so than either Hitler or Stalin.

Quote:
"I will build a car for the great multitude. It will be large enough for the family, but small enough for the individual to run and care for. It will be constructed of the best materials, by the best men to be hired, after the simplest designs that modern engineering can devise. But it will be low in price that no man making a good salary will be unable to own one - and enjoy with his family the blessing of hours of pleasure in God's great open spaces."

22.   James J. Hill

Born September 16th 1838 Died May 29th 1916 aged 77 Born in
what is now Ontario James J. Hill (he took the middle name of
Jerome for himself) was wounded as a child in an accident
with a bow and arrow which cost him the sight in his right eye.
He received nine years of education free, courtesy of the
headteacher at a local school and was talented at maths and
English.

He had to leave education on the death of his father, later
moving to Kentucky where he learned book keeping.
Deciding to stay in the US he settled in St Paul, Minnesota,
still only eighteen and worked as a book keeper for a
steamboat company. He then handled freight transfers for a
wholesale grocer which meant dealing with rail roads as well
as steamboat companies. In winter when the Mississippi was
frozen over he dabbled in his own entrepreneurial adventures.

Unable to fight in the civil war due to his sight problems he
nonetheless witnessed that terrible event and organised the 1st
Minnesota volunteers.

He entered both the coal and steamboat businesses on his own
account and managed to become a board member with several
banks. He came to monopolize the steamboat and coal
businesses locally and bought, rejuvenated and sold bankrupt
companies. With partners, since it would need an injection of
capital, he purchased the St Paul and Pacific Railroad,

a company he'd previously supplied with coal. This he extended driving rails across Minnesota and N. Dakota, ignoring the rights of native American Indians and getting the law changed later.

His railroad business became an empire and this is what he is mostly remembered for. Near the end of his life, together with J.P. Morgan he was one of the key instigators of the Anglo French Bond drive (1915) the resulting boom in munitions trade lifted the US out of recession and made 1915 and 1916 boom years.

23. George S. Parker

Born November 1st 1863 Died July 19th 1937 Although there were two famous George S. Parkers in Napoleon Hill's day he refers to George Safford Parker in his earlier writings and again in Think And Grow Rich. (The other was George Swinnerton Parker, founder of Parker Brothers games with brands such as Monopoly and Cluedo.)

Born in Wisconsin, George Safford Parker became a telegraphy operator who sold and repaired fountain pens as a sideline. He felt morally obliged to repair pens which leaked and invested in some basic tools. This led him to create a better pen, one that would both write better and not leak. He persuaded a local hotel, frequented by travelling salesmen, to stock his pens and one of them W.F. Palmer was so impressed he invested and The Parker Pen Company proper was launched.

The Parker pen company innovated in many ways, one illustration is their World War One Trench pen which used the cap as a mixing device whereby pills of solid ink could be added to water when needed.

24. E.M. Statler

Ellsworth Milton Statler, born October 26th 1863 died April 16th 1928

Aged twelve E.M. Statler worked in a glass factory. At thirteen he became a hotel bellboy and at fifteen was head bellboy. In 1896 he started his own restaurant with places for five hundred diners, it nearly bankrupted him, but through hard work and effective advertising he came through.

By 1901 (still only 37) he had amassed $60,000 in savings, his brother took over the restaurant and he went into the Hotel business. He built two hotels specifically for Expos which were torn down after the events. However, his first permanent hotel in Buffalo was pioneering, in having a bath or shower and running water in every guest room. And this was not a high price luxury hotel, this was a regular hotel for business travellers and tourists. The quote below provides an insight into the philosophy, one Napoleon Hill clearly espoused as well.

Further hotels were built by Statler during his lifetime, in Cleveland, Detroit, St. Louis and New York. More were constructed after his death and when the company was sold to Hilton in 1954 for $111 million it was the largest real estate transaction in history at that time.

Quote:

"Life is service. The one who progresses is the one who gives his fellow human beings a little more, a little better service."

25. Henry L. Doherty

Born May 15th 1870 Died December 26th 1939. Like so many of Napoleon Hill's heroes, Henry Latham Doherty was working at the age of twelve. In his case for the Columbus Gas Company. By twenty he was their Chief Engineer, before going to work for a financial company with utilities holdings.

The combination of technical and financial experience and skills led Doherty to form his own consulting business. He was pivotal in the growth of both the gas and electrical utilities and organised an effective sales force which contributed greatly to the spread of the necessary appliances. His Cities Service Co, built gas pipelines and organised stockpiles in times of low demand, they were organised. The company found gas and oil and became Citgo. The government forced the company to choose between oil and utilities and it ultimately went with oil.

Quote:

"The less you know how to do your work, the harder it is to do."

26. Cyrus H.K. Curtis

Born June 18th 1850 Portland Maine Died June 7th 1933 Wyncote, Pennsylvania. Left school in 1866 when the family home was destroyed in the Great fire of Portland and went to work in the field of advertising and newspapers. His own first publication was People's Ledger published weekly, initially in Boston.

In 1876 he relocated to Philadelphia Pennsylvania where he could achieve lower print costs. The Curtis publishing company went on to publish Ladies Home Journal, Saturday Evening Post and other titles whilst Curtis Martin Newspapers controlled the New York Evening Post, the Philadelphia Enquirer and others.

The huge success of the Ladies Home Journal was largely due in the first instance to the editorial brilliance of Curtis's wife Louisa Knapp, although it was continued by his son in law. To put Curtis's publishing empire in perspective, his fortune was estimated at 2008 values to have been $43.2 BILLION. Which would make him the 51st richest individual ever. Ahead even of J.P. Morgan.

Like Carnegie and others Curtis was a considerable philanthropist, dowering hospitals, museums, schools and universities and other institutions, a tradition carried on by his daughter.

27. Pres. Theodore Roosevelt

Born October 27th 1858 Died January 6th 1919 26th President of the USA. From a well to do family and widely regarded as one of the greatest American Presidents Teddy Roosevelt was in fact a sickly, asthmatic child who made himself strong with physical exercise and taking up pursuits such as boxing. His determination to make himself strong physically is a reflection of his mental strength and connects with Napoleon Hill's concept that thoughts are things and we are the products of our own minds.

By 1882 he was the youngest member of the New York State Assembly and clearly on the path to great things. However in 1884 tragedy struck when his wife and mother died on the same day. To heal his grief he became a rancher in the Dakota Badlands, drove cattle, hunted game and even outlaws, one of whom he captured. In 1886 he took a trip to London with his childhood friend Edith Carrow, they married there and Roosevelt ultimately returned to public life.

He was President of the New York Police Board 1895 – 1897 after which he became Assistant Secretary of the Navy.

He became a national hero in the Spanish American War, he resigned his position within the Naval administration and despite serving from May to September 1898 only, he quickly rose to the rank of Colonel in the Rough Rider's Regiment and led a famous uphill charge at the battle of San Juan. After his service, still in 1898 he became Governor of New York State. This lasted until 1900 and in 1901 he became Vice President to William McKinley. On September 6th that year McKinley was shot twice by an anarchist in the town of Buffalo. Initially it seemed McKinley would recover but in fact he passed away September 14th that year and Theodore Roosevelt became the youngest ever president of the USA, just before his 43rd birthday. Note JFK was the youngest person elected to the Presidency at 43 years of age. Teddy Roosevelt is the youngest to become president at 42 years of age. Bill Clinton was 46 and current President Obama 47.

Roosevelt is remembered for his 'square deal' and the Monroe Doctrine which said that the western hemisphere is off limits to foreign encroachment. Roosevelt added the corollary that it was the responsibility of America to intervene, with force if necessary, in Latin America to enforce the Monroe doctrine. See the famous 'big stick' quote below. He built up the US Navy and sent it off around the world on many visits to foreign countries to demonstrate America's power in the world.

Nonetheless he was also a worthy winner of the Nobel Peace Prize having mediated in the Russo Japanese war. He was additionally a conservationist, adding to national forests and taking a keen interest in irrigation projects. He didn't run in 1908 and took a famous safari after leaving office. He did campaign for the next term but lost out in the fight for the republican nomination to Taft. Typical of the man, he formed his own party (The Bull Moose Party) and ran anyway. He survived an assassination attempt while campaigning and finished ahead of Taft in the polls, but the split vote led to victory for Wilson.

He died in 1919 from coronary problems. After his failed attempt to regain the presidency he had undertaken an expedition to South America and contracted malaria, which had weakened him. He was just sixty when he passed away.

Quotes:

"The Constitution was made for the people and not the people for the Constitution."

"I wish that all Americans would realize that American politics is world politics."

"There is a homely adage which runs: 'Speak softly and carry a big stick; you will go far'. If the American nation will speak softly and yet build and keep at a pitch of the highest training a thoroughly efficient navy, the Monroe Doctrine will go far."

28. John W. Davis

Born April 13th 1873 Died March 24th 1955 His mother undertook his education until he reached the age of ten, when he did attend school and university he achieved outstanding grades. He was a remarkable lawyer arguing one hundred and forty cases before the US Supreme Court. He was a member of the House of Representatives, representing W Virginia 1911 – 1913 and US Solicitor General 1913 – 1918.

He made an unsuccessful bid for the presidency of the USA but was Ambassador to Great Britain under Woodrow Wilson. During his sixty year legal career he earned a reputation as one of the greatest advocates of his generation.

29. Elbert Hubbard

Born June 19th 1856   Died May 7th 1915 Remembered largely as an eccentric and a rebel (which he certainly was amongst other things), the life story of Elbert Green Hubbard is fascinating. Born on a farm he was at sixteen a soap salesman, and very good at it, ten years later he was number two in the company and had transformed the business, it no longer employed salesmen, but through his highly successful advertising and marketing had grown exponentially selling directly to customers through catalogs.

He married and had children but was not spiritually satisfied. His upbringing had been feverishly religious and he turned away from organised religion, believing that sermons came between him and God rather than bringing him closer. Eventually he sold up his stock options in Larkin soap. He was to found two businesses of his own, one was the Roycroft Press a publishing company which amongst other things published a magazine entitled The Philistine. It had a brown, butcher's paper cover, because said Hubbard it had meat inside. He was briefly stripped of his citizenship for misuse of the US Mail as it was considered in some quarters to be filth!

The second business was the Roycroft Arts and Crafts Community, it was the first and most successful arts and crafts business in the USA attracting and creating a community of artisans hammering copper, stitching leather and chiselling and planing wood. Amongst other things it made plain but artistic furniture in what was called Mission style after the early Spanish missions of that country's colonists. It was born from Hubbard's belief that machines were soulless and that industrialisation was dehumanising.

Hubbard's second wife was Alice Moore, she had been the family's lodger and although less pretty than Bertha, Hubbard found her more intellectually stimulating, she, like him was a fan of Emerson and as a champion of women's suffrage, she, like him, was something of a rebel. Bertha asked Alice to move away, which she did but after a long distance affair and innumerable letters Hubbard ultimately married Alice. She was his soulmate.

A prolific writer Hubbard eulogised a Mr and Mrs Straus a couple who were aboard the ill fated Titanic. As a woman Mrs Straus was entitled to a place in a lifeboat, but preferred to die with the husband she loved and declined to leave him.

Ironically, pardoned for his perceived indiscretion with 'The Philistine' Woodrow Wilson sent Hubbard to Europe to cover the war. He had ambitions to interview the Kaiser. However, they travelled aboard the Lusitania, which on , May 7th 1915 was torpedoed in the Irish Sea by a German U Boat (submarine). It was reported that on seeing their plight was hopeless Elbert and Alice shut themselves in a nearby cabin in order that they should die together and their bodies not become separated in the water.

Quotes:

"A friend is one who knows you and loves you just the same."

"A failure is a man who has blundered, but is not able to cash in the experience."

30. Wilbur Wright

Born April 16th 1867 Died May 30th 1912 Despite claims and counter claims the Wright brothers are generally credited with making the first heavier than air powered flight with Wilbur being the pilot on that first flight. His was a short life full of adventure. Although historians generally agree that Wilbur was the driving force behind the airplane project both brothers shared the credit equally. Wilbur was the older of the brothers Orville being born August 19th 1871, died January 30th 1948.

As children the boys were inspired by a toy brought back from his travels by their father who was a bishop. It was a kind of helicopter toy developed in France and made from paper, bamboo and cork. They played with it until it broke then made their own version. As a young man Wilbur was accidentally struck by a hockey stick, he lost some teeth and became withdrawn, he nursed his terminally ill mother and assisted his father with problems at the church. Although he did not attend Yale as planned he did read extensively in his father's library.

The two brothers formed a business, they did some printing but bicycling was the new craze so they got into the a bicycle repair and exchange business with a small shop and later built their own brand of bicycle. In the mid 1890's the first aeronautical developments were attracting public interest there had been unmanned flights by what we would today consider to be model aircraft, even a steam powered one and various pioneers were making short flights with various types of glider. Sadly some of these pioneers lost their lives, not so much because the gliders didn't work as because they could not be adequately controlled.

In 1899 after reading all the material they could get hold of, the Wright brothers started work in earnest. They built a number of kites and gliders and initially Wilbur was the one who flew in the glider, possibly because he had initiated the project and felt a responsibility towards his younger brother. Eventually Orville was gliding too. The brothers concentrated their efforts on how to control their craft. When others were trying to make their craft turn flat like a boat the Wright brothers had already understood the need for an aircraft to bank into the turn like a bird.

They built their aircraft in the cycle shop from spruce frames with a fabric covering and had a gasoline engine built there by one of their employees in consultation with others when existing manufacturers could not make an engine light enough. The aero engine they built had an aluminum block and an early form of fuel injection using gravity feed and no carburettor. It was created in approximately six weeks!

The Wright brothers laminated wooden propellers were developed by themselves and have been tested in more modern times and found to be extremely efficient. They used two, counter rotating to cancel torque, truly they were ahead of their time. Their first heavier than air, manned flight took place on December 17th 1903, their pioneering development work over the next two years was later recognised although at the time, particularly in France their claims were met with scepticism if not downright hostility. In 1904 and 1905 they made their machine into a practical flying machine. They were more or less ignored by the media, something they probably actively strove to achieve as they did not want their ideas stolen.

No flights were undertaken by them in 1906 and 1907 although their flyer II and flyer III had achieved the feat of flying circles and figure eights in the previous two years, the wings being distorted by the controls to achieve the banking effect. Not everything they tried worked and there were some, thankfully non fatal, accidents. During 1906 and 7 the brothers concentrated on negotiating contracts with the US and other governments.

In 1908 Wilbur took one flying machine to France to demonstrate while Orville demonstrated a similar, but not identical machine at home in the US. In France where Wilbur demonstrated circles and figure of eight manoeuvres all his doubters were silenced and he received many accolades and apologies for past accusations of false claims. In the US Orville achieved the first flight of over an hour in a demonstration to the US military. Before long they were taking passengers, this being a requirement of the military and sadly Orville crashed when a propeller split in flight. He himself was hospitalised for some seven weeks with numerous broken bones, his passenger a US Army observer died the evening of the crash, becoming the first air crash fatality in history.

When asked in hospital if he might lose his nerve Orville replied "the only thing I'm afraid of is that I can't get well soon enough to finish those tests next year" Wilbur, still demonstrating in France was spurred on to set new records for altitude and duration. When recovered Orville joined Wilbur in France together with their sister Katherine. They became the most famous people on the planet, being fêted by royalty, the rich, the media and the public.

In 1909 the brothers sold their first airplane to the US military for $30,000, which included a $5,000 bonus for exceeding the speed requirement laid down in the performance requirements. That same year Wilbur flew around the Statue of Liberty. Wilbur had previously taken Katherine for a flight and on one occasion only, with their father's permission the two brothers flew together. Their father Milton had not wanted to risk losing both sons, nor would he have wanted their pioneering work to halt as it would have done had both his sons perished in an accident. Now however Orville took Milton, at the age of 82, aloft, the old gentleman shouting ecstatically "higher Orville higher!"

In business the brothers became rich, but patent lawsuits tarnished their reputation as national heroes. One litigant claiming a man would only have to jump in the air and flap his arms to be sued by the Wright brothers. However, they trained Henry 'Hap' Arnold, who would go on to be the first head of the US air force, to fly and Eddie Stinson, the founder of the Stinson aircraft company.

Wilbur tragically died of Typhoid aged just 45, neither brother ever married. Orville sold the company in 1915, he, Katherine and their father Milton moved in to a large mansion. Wilbur Wright's short life was filled with incident and achievement as expressed so eloquently by his father, see the quote below.

Others have claimed to have flown before the Wright brothers, some have claimed (ludicrously in the view of this author) that the use of a headwind negates the achievement or claim to the first powered flight, or that the use of rails to control take off somehow negates the record. Some have claimed others did it earlier than December 17th 1903 and some say the record should go to flights made in still conditions, without rails made after 1903. Whatever view you take there is no doubt that the Wright brothers did it their way and that their pioneering work on making an aircraft that could be banked, turned and controlled truly started mankind on the pathway to the mastery of the air. Their vision, courage, hard work and their success mark them out as amongst the truly great human beings of the 20th century, their aircraft mark a huge milestone in human endeavour and achievement.

Quote by Milton Wright

> *"May 30, 1912*
>
> *This morning at 3:15, Wilbur passed away, aged 45 years, 1 month, and 14 days.*
>
> *A short life, full of consequences.*
>
> *An unfailing intellect, imperturbable temper, great self-reliance and as great modesty, seeing the right clearly, pursuing it steadily, he lived and died.*
>
> *- Bishop Milton Wright"*

31. William Jennings Bryan

Born March 19th 1860 – Died July 26th 1925 His father had been a member of the Illinois State Senate and a circuit judge, so it's perhaps unsurprising that William Jennings Bryan too became a politician. Reckoned to be one of the most popular speakers in American history, it was not enough to see him elected President despite winning the Democratic nomination no less than three times.

He was elected to Congress in the democratic landslide of 1890 and was re-elected in 1892. He championed the common man, believing in the goodness of ordinary people and wanted to regulate the railways and bust the powerful trusts (monopolies). His attitude towards the people earned him the nickname 'The Great Commoner'.

Appointed Secretary of State by Woodrow Wilson, he later resigned the post in protest at Wilson's handling of the Lusitania disaster and subsequent political crisis. He was a supporter of prohibition and no admirer of Napoleon Hill's hero Darwin, campaigning against the teaching of evolution in schools. He was a believer in World Peace and felt that German Militarism was based on Darwinian principles of survival of the fittest, and natural selection, which had led to a might is right attitude.

He was a tireless worker, campaigner and litigant in order to try and influence home and world affairs. This probably led to his death, he died peacefully in his sleep, brought on apparently by the combination of diabetes and fatigue. He was a committed Presbyterian Christian.

32. Dr David Starr Jordan

In Napoleon Hill's list of influential people there appears a Dr Dmtid Starr Jordan. This is a misprint or typographical error for Dr David Starr Jordan, who is exactly the sort of person Hill would have admired. If you need convincing see the choices he made for his imaginary council.

Dr Jordan was born January 19th 1851 – Died September 19th 1931 Once described as the most influential of American ichthyologists Dr Jordan would have attracted Napoleon Hill's interest for both his outstanding achievements in natural history and academia as well as for his ethics.

President of Indiana University at 34 he was the nation's youngest University President. During the course of his career he would also be President of Stanford and a prolific writer, publishing amongst many others Fishes of North and Middle America (in four volumes), War and Waste, and Ways of Lasting Peace.

He led scientific expeditions to far flung places such as the volcanic Pribilof Islands off Alaska and was President of The World Peace Foundation 1910 – 1914.

33. J. Ogden Armour

Born November 11th 1863 – Died August 16th 1927 Jonathon
Ogden Armour is listed in the Author's Preface of Think And
Grow Rich, while his father Philip D. Armour Born 16th May
1832 – Died 6th January 1901 is referred to later in connection
with Dr Gunsaulus and the Armour Institute of Technology.
We will provide a snapshot of both here. Philip Danforth
Armour founded Armour & Company, with partners. It was a
meatpacking company that would become a giant food
company under his son's stewardship.

Initially the elder Armour took over the company and it was
he who donated the money to Dr Gunsaulus to found the
Armour Institute of Technology, today called the Illinois
Institute of Technology.

J Ogden Armour took over the company after the death of his
father and the premature death of his younger brother. He
transformed it from a company turning over $200 million into
one turning over $1 billion. He broke a major strike by
employing thousands of unemployed African Americans,
sparking a riot, but he won. He defeated a trust breaking suit
brought by the government against his company and several
others when he convinced his co-defendants to let the case go
before a jury having offered no defense.

He appeared in the Forbes rich list and had interests in power and light, railroads and aviation. After selling bonds in World War One Armour and Company became the first meatpacking company to be publicly listed. J. Ogden Armour also published two books 'The Packers, The Private Car Lines and The People', and 'Business Problems of the War'.

He was ideally placed to pen the latter, he lost millions, some say a million dollars a day for one hundred and thirty days! Nonetheless, when he died of a heart attack in London his shares in Universal Oil alone were worth $3million.

Quote:

"I lost money so fast, I didn't think it was possible."

34. Harris F. Williams

Given Napoleon Hill's connections with distance learning in Chicago it seems likely this name in the list near the beginning of Think And Grow Rich refers to the Harris F. Williams who was the author of 'Chicago Correspondence Schools – Business Course – Commercial Law' published 1903.

The same name appears as an advocate in court cases of the period. A Harris F. Williams born March 1 1869 at Springfield Mo later attended the University of Chicago and was admitted to the Bench and Bar of Illinois in 1894.

35. Dr Frank Gunsaulus

Born January 1st 1856 – Died March 17th 1921 Dr Frank Wakeley Gunsaulus was a preacher, educator, author and humanitarian. The million dollar sermon story Napoleon Hill tells us gives us a measure of the man. He was born of Spanish immigrant stock on one side of the family and Dutch on the other. His father was a republican politician and became Mayor of Chesterville for many years.

Frank Gunsaulus attended public schools and then the Ohio Weslyan University, his classmates and professors were amazed by the power of his oratory, he was also a voracious reader, particularly the classics by various accounts and had an amazing memory. He authored some fifteen books mostly concerning history, religion and poetry although his biography of Gladstone may be the kind of thing that would be of particular interest to readers of Hill's Heroes.

36. Daniel Willard

Born January 28th 1861 – Died July 6th 1942 Daniel Willard was descended from one of the earliest English colonists of the 1600s. Like many other of Hill's heroes he had a less than ideal education, cut short by relative poverty and in his case poor eyesight. Nonetheless he would eventually become a trustee and Chairman of the Board of John Hopkins University.

He is best remembered as the President of The Baltimore and Ohio Railroad, a position he held from 1910 to 1941. He served on several government commissions during World War I and made the cover of Time Magazine for his role in wage cutting during the Great Depression.

37. King Gillette

Born January 5th 1855 – Died July 9th 1932 King Camp Gillette is widely credited as the inventor of the safety razor, which isn't strictly true. What he did do is invent a safety razor with disposable blades and that revolutionized the way men shaved and made him a fortune.

Raised in Chicago Gillette's family were devastated by the Great Fire of 1871. He became a salesman selling cork seals for bottles. Seeing how the product he sold was frequently discarded he made the mental leap, understanding the public desire for cheap disposable convenience items, that led him to the idea for a safety razor where the blades could be used until dull then thrown away and replaced.

A form of safety razor already existed but it used an expensive forged blade, as did the 'cut throat' razor barbers used and sharpened on a leather strop. It took Gillette several years before he found an engineer who could produce what he wanted, however, he ended up with his sheet steel disposable blade. It was his thinking, backed by persistence that made him rich.

He was a utopian and a socialist and wrote several books, including 'The Human Drift' and 'The People's Corporation'. He travelled extensively and was widely recognised due to his picture appearing on the packs of razor blades. People were amazed to find it was really him and not just a marketing image.

The Great Depression brought him to the verge of bankruptcy, yet today the brand he launched is still number one in the shaving market.

38. Ralph A. Weeks

In 1929, after a year of driving for Ridge Road Express - Ralph A. Weeks purchased the company…a two-bus operation based in Jeddo, NY.

With Mr. Weeks behind the wheel of a 15 passenger 1927 Garford bus and Mrs. Weeks driving a seven-passenger Buick Sedan, Ridge Road Express began its first regularly scheduled line run, offering service between Lockport and Lyndonville NY along Ridge Road (Route 104).

But, as times changed, so did the company and today nearly 80 percent of our current operation is carrying students. With 300 buses and vans serving 10 school districts, Ridge Road Express safely transports 3.6 million students per year.

In 1935, the Weeks family purchased Grand Island Transit Corporation (GITC), an inter-city bus line offering service between Buffalo and Niagara Falls, NY across Grand Island. Over the years, GITC evolved into a full-service deluxe charter and tour motorcoach company now known as Grand Tours.

39. Judge Daniel Thew Wright

Born in Riverside Ohio on September 24th 1864 Daniel Thew Wright qualified in law at the University Of Cincinnati College Of Law became a prosecuting attorney and went on to become Mayor of Riverside from 1890 to 1893.

He was appointed a Federal Judge in the US district court for the District of Columbia (Supreme Court of the District of Columbia) in 1903. His appointment was opposed by Senator Hanna and one George B. Cox on the grounds that he had not been a regular supporter of the Republican Organization of Cincinnati. the complaints were investigated by the Attorney General who could find nothing against his character or fitness for the position.

He resigned in 1914 and finished his career in private practice having also been adjunct professor at Georgetown University.

In 1908 Judge Wright had a famous conflict with another of Hill's Heroes, labor leader Samuel Gompers, who would go on to describe the judge as unfit. Gompers and others were found to be in contempt of court for violating an injunction restraining labor union leaders from a boycott in the 'Buck's Stove case'. In 1911 the supreme Court reversed the decision and the following day Judge Wright instigated new proceedings. The dispute dragged on but a new president of the Buck's Stove Company eventually reached an agreement with the workers which ended the saga.

Judge Wright died in 1943 in Fenwick Maryland.

40. John D. Rockefeller

Born July 8th 1839 - Died May 23rd 1937 Oil industry magnate, ruthless, self made businessman with a philanthropic streak who was considered a public enemy by many in his lifetime, but died a popular figure.

John Davison Rockefeller was the second child of Eliza Davison and William Avery Rockefeller, known as Big Bill by the more charitable and Devil Bill by the straight talkers. John D. had five siblings. He was raised a Northern Baptist by his mother. His father was largely absent, a philanderer, bigamist and something of a snake oil salesman, by which I mean he sold curative elixirs of dubious nature and was sharp at best, fraudulent more likely. John D. Rockefeller clearly learnt from both parents, no sooner was John employed at a meagre 50 cents a day than he gave 6%
of his earnings away to charity, or church rising to 10% as his wages increased. However, in business on his own account not long after he ruthlessly drove competitors to bankruptcy when they declined to sell to him. This trait was probably borne of his father's contribution to the young man's upbringing, for while John helped his mother with the chores, demonstrated devout tendencies and entrepreneurial ones, raising and selling turkeys, and selling candy to his contemporaries, his father bragged "I cheat my boys every chance I get. I want to make 'em sharp!"

Nonetheless the youthful John was variously described as being religious, reserved, earnest, discreet and methodical. He also displayed a love of music and debate in both of which activities he showed early promise. He had a very good head for figures. The family moved frequently but a large portion of John's education was at Owego Academy after which he got his 50 cents a day job with Hewitt & Tuttle. His role there was book keeping, whilst the company business was what was known as produce and commission, which is to say selling farm implements, fertilizers and household goods. Rockefeller's first foray into business on his own account would be in the same business with an English partner Maurice B. Clark, together they raised $4,000 in capital and succeeded in turning a profit each and every year including the first. Indeed that first year their turnover was half a million dollars! Rockefeller was the office manager and book keeper whilst Clark was the 'people person' handling both buying and selling.

In 1863 the pair invested their profits in the building of an oil refinery in partnership with Clark's brothers James and Richard and one Samuel Adams. The company was called Andrews, Clark & Company but Andrews and Rockefeller bought the Clarks out two years later. The Clark's then formed the rival company of Clark, Payne & Co which in 1872 would be merged into Rockefeller's burgeoning Standard Oil.

Let's just stop and put this in perspective for a moment. The oil industry was in its infancy, the internal combustion engine was actually invented in 1863 the same year Rockefeller and partners began building their first refinery, but Karl Benz widely acclaimed as the father of the automobile would not show a three wheeler until 1885, a four wheeler following in 1886, some 23 years after Rockefeller entered the oil business – so why get into oil? To understand how large the lighting oil business was I suggest reading Melville's excellent Moby Dick. However, whale oil was becoming too costly for many ordinary people and Hill's Hero Thomas Edison had yet to electrify the world's households. Edison wasn't technically first to produce an electric light bulb but he was the first to produce one that would last, the year 1879, sixteen years after Rockefeller's first refinery was built and it would take many more years for electrification to spread, across America and the world. Therefore in many ways it was kerosene for use in oil lamps that launched Rockefeller on the path to world's richest man. Then in 1908 Hill's Hero Henry Ford launched his Model T automobile and made motoring, through the invention of assembly line production, accessible to the masses. The famous gasoline brand (petrol to the British) ESSO is simply the phonetic spelling of Standard Oil.

Back to the story of John D. Rockefeller's life. While John's brother Frank fought in the civil war John, like many wealthy northerners gave money to the Union cause. He was a lifelong supporter of the then fledgling Republican Party, a strong supporter of Abraham Lincoln, a leading abolitionist, that is to say anti slavery and true to his mother's teachings and Baptist beliefs he was also later a contributor to the funds of the Anti Saloon League and therefore party to the misguided experiment that was abolition. Another brother, William built a new refinery in 1867 and brought John and Henry M. Flagler into partnership with him, this company being Rockefeller, Andrews & Flagler, the forerunner of Standard Oil. Although Standard Oil was formally created in 1870 by 1868 they already had the largest oil refinery in the world.

Rockefeller had learned much about the impact of transportation costs in the produce and commission business. He formed a cartel with others to obtain beneficial rates from the railroads and the savings enabled him to undercut his competitors. A storm of protest from smaller players and the media led in time to the railroads creating fixed tariffs but Rockefeller was still making secret deals behind closed doors wherever possible and undercutting rivals. In what was to become known as The Cleveland Massacre, Standard Oil took over twenty two of twenty six competitors in Cleveland in just a four month period during 1872.

Standard Oil went into competition, in fact a trade war, with the railroads by building pipelines, which led to the railroads buying into the oil industry. Standard also supplied kerosene to local markets in its own 'Tank Cars'. The company's innovative side didn't end there however, they invented more than three hundred new oil based products including chewing gum (see Hill's Hero W.M. Wrigley Jnr.), vaseline, tar and paint.

Meanwhile Rockefeller's war of conquest continued apace, he would make a practice of showing his books to competitors at the same time making them an offer backed by the threat that if they didn't sell then he would run them into bankruptcy and purchase their assets cheaply at auction. Some references suggest that he made a habit of making a fair initial offer, we're somewhat removed now and unable to be certain of the veracity of that claim, certainly businesses that declined to sell were battered into submission and later court hearings and conclusions suggest Rockefeller was not devoid of either his father's genes or some of his 'sharp' practices. The company gradually achieved virtually complete control of the oil industry in the U.S., becoming the richest, biggest and most feared company in the world.

Standard Oil sparked much public and political unrest. It formed a 'trust' which was effectively what today would be called a holding company and at one point in the 1880s its share of world refining went as high as 90%, at which time it owned 20,000 domestic oil wells, 4,000 miles of pipeline, 5,000 'tank cars' and it employed in excess of one hundred thousand people.

In the 1890s the company expanded into iron ore, bringing it into competition with another of Hill's Heroes, Andrew Carnegie. However, Rockefeller himself would soon retire and another of Hill's Heroes, Theodore Roosevelt would use the Sherman Anti-Trust Act to initiate law suits against the company. Yet another of Hill's Heroes J.P. Morgan, having bought Carnegie's steel assets exchanged Standard Oil's iron interests for stock in U.S. Steel, Rockefeller and his son obtaining seats on the board of that company and bringing that potential war to a halt.

It was not until 1911 two years after the launch of the Model T Ford that the law suits against Standard bore fruit and the 'monopoly' was broken up into thirty four companies. Despite the court finding that the company originated in illegal monopoly practices all shareholders, including Rockefeller and his son were given proportional stocks in the new companies. The stocks duly rose five fold within ten years.

The first American to become a dollar billionaire in 1916, Rockefeller's wealth probably peaked at $1.5 billion and was still $1.4 billion on death which in 2000 figures could be as much as $663 billion. He was at one time worth 1.53% of the entire U.S. economy. Although a famed philanthropist the proportion of his wealth left intact on death is in stark contrast to that of Hill's Hero Andrew Carnegie, his contemporary, rival and the second richest man in modern history. Nonetheless it's not simply a matter of subtracting Rockefeller's wealth at death from his wealth at it's peak, naturally he enjoyed a huge income over many years and it's not inconceivable that his philanthropic donations over his entire life were as much as $550 million.

Philanthropy is defined as the effort or inclination to increase the well being of humankind and derives from the ancient Greek Myth of Prometheus. Certainly Rockefeller demonstrated this tendency early in his working life. His donations to good causes, particularly medical research were instrumental in ridding the world of Hookworm and Yellow Fever. He adopted a systematic approach of targeted giving which has been copied by other major philanthropists and he founded in effect both the University of Chicago and The Rockefeller University.

It can be seen from this section just how the lives of many of Hill's Heroes impinged on one another and affected the outcomes; possibly a strong argument in favour of a Master Mind, their influence on our lives today is quite incredible with men like Rockefeller, Carnegie, Edison and Ford toward the forefront. The proportion of his wealth that Rockefeller gave to good causes fell as his wealth ballooned, in contrast to Andrew Carnegie, but his effect on our world should not be underestimated.

Several of the quotes below support assertions in Think and Grow Rich concerning persistence, thinking outside the box (in modern terminology), a goal beyond mere riches for riches' sake and singleness of purpose, others are just good sound business advice and can be identified with Rockefeller's strategy in business as told in his story above.

Quotes:

'the riches available to man are practically without limit, that the world's wealth is constantly being developed and undergoing mutation, and that to promote this process both Labor and Capital are indispensable. If these great forces cooperate, the products of industry are steadily increased; whereas, if they fight, the production of wealth is certain to be either retarded or stopped altogether and the wellsprings of material progress choked.'

"A friendship founded on business is better than a business founded on friendship."

"Charity is injurious unless it helps the recipient to become independent of it."

"Every right implies a responsibility; Every opportunity, an obligation, Every possession, a duty."

"I do not think that there is any other quality so essential to success of any kind as the quality of perseverance. It overcomes almost everything, even nature."

"If you want to succeed you should strike out on new paths, rather than travel the worn paths of accepted success."

"Singleness of purpose is one of the chief essentials for success in life, no matter what may be one's aim."

"The way to make money is to buy when blood is running in the streets."

"If your only goal is to become rich, you will never achieve it."

41. Frank A. Vanderlip

Born November 17th 1864 – Died June 30th 1937. Frank A. Vanderlip was born in Aurora Illinois and raised on a farm. Although he attended the University of Illinois as a young man he was unable to finish the course and was apprenticed to a machine shop in Aurora. The University of Illinois later awarded him an honorary Master of Arts degree in recognition of his writings on financial matters. Whilst working as a machine operator Vanderlip continued to study both mechanics and shorthand, which skill he practised using chalk on the bed plate of his machine.

Seeing no future for himself in Aurora, at age around twenty, Vanderlip set out for Chicago where he initially found work with a firm making financial reports for corporations. This led to a position reporting on financial matters for the Chicago Tribune and due to the quality and clarity of his work he soon became Financial Editor. despite this recognition and success Vanderlip continued to study, this time at the University of Chicago where he took a course in political economy. He bought a share in The Economist magazine and became one of its editors.

The Secretary Of The Treasury in President McKinley's cabinet made Vanderlip his Private Secretary and after a mere two months in the post he was made Assistant Secretary Of The Treasury in which role he negotiated a $200 million loan from the National City Bank to finance the government's Spanish – American War of 1898. After four years of government service he resigned to join the aforementioned bank as Vice President.

Prior to taking up his new position Vanderlip embarked on a tour of Europe to study European financial systems and economies, writing a series of articles for Scribner's Magazine entitled The American 'Commercial Invasion' Of Europe subsequently published in book form. He later penned another book Business and Education and in 1909 became President of the National city Bank, today known as Citibank. He additionally served on the boards of numerous major corporations of the era including The Union Pacific Railroad and Consolidated Gas.

In common with so many of Hill's Heroes Vanderlip worked to help others, he was a trustee of the Carnegie Foundation For The Advancement Of Teaching and was personally responsible for the adoption of the Montessori Method of Kindergarten Education by the first American school to offer it. He was also president of the board of managers of an institution to help those with learning disabilities.

42. Edward A. Filene

Born September 3rd 1860 – Died September 26th 1937 Born in Salem Massachusetts to Clara Ballin and William Filene, a Jewish immigrant from Posen, in Prussia, today the fifth largest town in Poland, Filene was one of five children. He was a bright scholar and passed his entrance exams for Harvard, an opportunity he was never able to take up. When his father became seriously ill, he and his younger brother Abraham Lincoln Filene took over the running of the family business comprising several small stores in ladies'clothing and a fledgling department store in Boston. If he gave up his goal of going to Harvard from a sense of duty he nonetheless made Filene's Department Store one of the giants of U.S. retailing.

Filene studied methods being promulgated at the time by one Frederick Winslow Taylor to improve workplace efficiency, but Filene's own innovations are largely responsible for the success and fame of Filene's Department Store. He set out to provide both a complete and honest description of every item sold in his store and backed it up with a money back guarantee based on satisfaction, not merely guaranteeing against faulty goods. The Boston public loved it. They warmed further to Filene's Bargain Basement. Launched in 1909 this was not the first bargain basement in the U.S., however he instigated a system of automatic knock-downs with time, a sort of reverse auction, it created excitement and profit.

Not only an astute businessman Filene can equally be described as an innovator, a social engineer, a philanthropist, a deep thinker and a man of action. In his business he instigated practices that were way ahead of his time such as a forty hour week, health clinics and paid vacations and a minimum wage for women. He formed a savings and loan association for his employees and engaged in collective bargaining and arbitration in preference to confrontation; indeed he believed that ordinary people must prosper in order to be able to buy the products modern methods pioneered by the likes of Hill's Hero Henry Ford had made available in quantity. The quote below illustrates his belief in the interdependency of all Americans for the general well being.

Ironically Filene himself lived modestly and never owned an automobile. However, he did travel widely and corresponded with world leaders such as Hill's Heroes Woodrow Wilson and Mahatma Gandhi. He also exchanged letters with Franklin D. Roosevelt and the Russian Marxist leader Vladimir Ilyich Lenin.

At home he was involved in private sector/public sector partnerships endeavouring to solve the age old problems of crime, slums, public health, and proper governance. He was possibly responsible for coining the term Credit Union, though it was from looking at British practices in India that he drew his inspiration. He was a campaigner for the Massachusetts Credit Union Act of 1909 that led to the Federal credit union Act of 1934.

A childhood injury had given Filene a lifelong limp, which combined with youthful eczema was probably at the root of his shyness, a seemingly unlikely trait in one who was one of the movers and shakers of his age. To support that statement it should be noted that by 2008 there were 89 million individual members of credit unions in the U.S. Filene never married and ultimately the store was swallowed up by the Macy's empire. The external façade of the original Boston building is preserved although other elegant stores and the beautiful panelled interior of the original are lost. Filene himself is commemorated in a number of busts and plaques and buildings named for him, but most fittingly for this inquisitive traveller and deep thinker, who died in Paris, France, the think tank The Filene Research Institute is also named after him.

Quote:

"What is needed is that the American masses shall learn the art of constructive self-government in this machine age – in this age in which life is no longer organized on a small community pattern but in which all Americans are more or less dependent upon what all other Americans are doing."

43. Edwin C. Barnes

Born 1878 – Died September 23rd 1952. Details about Edwin C. Barnes are scarce. Was he one of the great men of his age, a mover and shaker who changed the world? No he was not or we would know a deal more about him. Did he play his part? He most certainly did. We know something of the senior officers who accompanied Caesar for example. He changed his world, but he did not do it alone. Edwin C. Barnes too played his role in history. Most of what we know about Barnes however comes from Napoleon Hill's writings. I believe Barnes himself would be surprised how much interest his story still generates today.

An examination of Thomas Edison's life and papers will reveal a great list of companies he founded or was a partner or director of. Edwin C. Barnes was effectively his partner in one arena the Ediphone dictation machine. The veracity of Hill's story regarding Barnes is not in question. Some would have described Barnes as a 'down and out' when he arrived at Edison's premises in Orange. By this time Edison was already a great man. Barnes' arrival with the faintly ridiculous suggestion that he'd come to be the great man's partner probably made others snigger. I prefer to see Barnes as 'down but not out', persistence as one of the great lessons we need to learn, and that is what makes Barnes' story so special. A person may be down, but they're not out until they give up.

There is a photograph extant showing a dapper young Barnes in a stylish suit, good shoes and smart haircut in the company of the old man. When he died in 1952 Barnes was a multi millionaire, he had started with a dream, visualised and believed in it, formed a strategy and persisted until it was a reality. He worked until the year before his death retiring in 1951 and spending time in Florida, New York and Maine.

44. Arthur Brisbane

Born December 12th 1864 – Died December 25th 1936. Arthur Brisbane was born in Buffalo, New York State near the shore of Lake Eyrie, the son of Albert Brisbane a socialist writer who wrote a column in The New York Tribune, edited a socialist 'parlor magazine' and wrote a book entitled The Social Destiny Of Man. Hill's Hero Arthur would go on to be described as the greatest journalist of his day by the famous publisher William Randolph Hearst. Arthur Brisbane would also be described as a liberal turned conservative.

Educated in both Europe and the U.S. Brisbane's journalistic career began in 1882 as a reporter for The Sun newspaper in New York, from there he went to Joseph Pulitzer's, new at the time, publication New York World and from there was head-hunted by Hearst and worked initially as editor of New York Journal, circa 1897, and then the flagship publication of the Hearst empire the Evening Journal. The relationship with Hearst became very important to Brisbane both business wise and personally, the two men forming a deep personal friendship as well as collaborating in many things such as property investments and purchasing and turning around failing publications. Hearst would write a moving obituary on Brisbane's death.

Brisbane's work was hugely popular and widely syndicated, his influence far reaching. Time magazine estimated he had thirty million regular readers, his 'This Week' column was syndicated in twelve hundred weekly papers whilst two hundred daily papers took hi 'Today' column. He interviewed presidents and many of the great men and women of his day. His salary reached $260 thousand per annum in the thirties and he made much more from his real estate investments and joint ventures in publishing. Volumes of his work were also published in book form such as 'The Book Of Today' and 'The Book Of Today And Tomorrow'. There are also two books by Brisbane on Mary Baker Eddy the founder of the Christian science movement and one on advertising.

Other interests included boxing and horses. Brisbane built a large mansion with an impressive library in a tower at Allaire on the New Jersey Shore, it was a playground for his family and had a state of the art horse farm. However he also preserved an historic iron working village from the 19th century and allowed his estate to be used for Boy Scout camps, silent movie backdrops and as a training ground in World War Two.

On his death the family home became a child care center and much of the estate was left to the State of New Jersey, including that part containing the historic village, with the stipulation that it be used only for historic and forest preservation purposes. The public still benefits from it today.

The first quote below is of especial interest to readers of Hill's Heroes the others demonstrate his professional ability and sense of humor.

Quotes:

"Regret for time wasted can become a power for good in the time that remains, if we will only stop the waste and the idle, useless regretting."

"If you don't hit the reader between the eyes in your first sentence of your news column, there's no need to write any more,"

"A good friend can tell you what is the matter with you in a minute. He may not seem such a good friend after telling."

"Whatever good there is in small boys is usually based upon their admiration for girls of their own age"

"The fence around a cemetery is foolish, for those inside can't get out and those outside don't want to get in."

"Writing good editorials is chiefly telling the people what they think, not what you think."

45. Luther A. Burbank

Born 7th March 1849 – Died 11th April 1926 If the human species has failed to properly feed all on the planet the blame for that cannot be laid at the door of Luther Burbank, whilst the possibility that we might one day do so, is in no small measure due to his fifty five years of hard patient work as a botanist, horticulturist and one of the pioneers of agricultural science.

Burbank developed in excess of eight hundred strains and varieties of plant including potatoes, grains, cattle feed plants, fruits, nuts and vegetables, and flowers for our enjoyment too.

Born in Lancaster, Massachusetts, Burbank was the thirteenth child of fifteen and received only a rudimentary education. His father died when he was twenty one and he invested his inheritance into seventeen acres of land near Lunenburg, Massachusetts where he developed his first product, the Burbank potato. He sold the rights to his new potato to one J.H. Gregory who in fact gave it its original name Burbank Seedling. With the $150 dollars he received for his new variety of potato and ten tubers Gregory allowed him to keep, Burbank set off for California, settling at Santa Rosa. By 1906 six million bushels of the Burbank potato had been produced across California, Oregon and Washington from Burbank's ten examples.

A Colorado man produced a mutant variety today known as the Burbank Russet potato which is potato blight resistant and the mainstay of the food processing and fast food industry where it is the potato of choice for most of the 'French Fries' produced in the USA. Burbank acknowledged the improvement but his own career was to produce so much more.

In Santa Rosa Burbank purchased four acres and set up a greenhouse and nursery. His experiments there being inspired by the writings of Charles Darwin and where he was supported financially by another of Hill's Heroes Andrew Carnegie, despite Carnegie's own advisers believing that Burbank's methods were insufficiently scientific. (They were however practical and got results which no doubt appealed to Carnegie!) Burbank experimented with grafting, hybridization and cross breeding and produced many incredibly useful and in some cases beautiful plants, too many to list here, but including not just higher yields for humans, but even a spineless cactus for cattle feed in the more arid regions. Despite the criticism of some in the scientific community, today less well remembered Burbank did catalog his work and he authored several books.

His success at Santa Rosa enabled him to purchase a further eighteen acres named Gold Ridge Farm at nearby Sebastopol, where much more work could be done. Work that influenced the Plant Patent Act which would be passed four years after Burbank's death, a bill that was supported by Hill's Hero the great inventor Thomas Edison. Several patents were awarded to Burbank posthumously, whilst Edison said of the Act "This bill, will, I feel sure, give us many Burbanks".

Burbank's widow donated the greater part of Gold Ridge Farm to Sebastopol for low income housing to be erected, but the caretaker's cottage and two hundred and fifty living examples of Burbank's work are today cared for by volunteers. Both the housing and the living memorial are fitting for a man who lived modestly whilst improving the lives of all of us and giving generously to local schools. (Several places of education are today named after him). The house and gardens at Santa Rosa are also preserved and open to the public, whilst the house Burbank was born in, together with his California garden office were moved by another Hill's Hero, Henry Ford to be preserved for posterity at Greenfield Village, Dearborn, Michigan.

The work of Burbank is too vast in scope to portray adequately here, but as an example let us look at the story of the Shasta Daisy, so named by Burbank in honor of the snowy peak of the California mountain. As a boy Burbank was inspired by a love of the Oxeye daisy, a hardy European flower accidentally imported to New England by the Pilgrim Fathers and seen by most as a weed and a menace. Burbank saw the potential and the beauty of the wild flower but he wished to improve its size and whiteness, the broadness of its petals and he wanted it to bloom early and persistently in order that it become a loved garden flower rather than being perceived as a weed. It took Burbank fifteen years of hard labor to achieve all his goals, painstakingly brushing pollen from other daisy varieties from around the world on to the best of each year's blooms, thousands, possibly hundreds of thousands of them until he achieved what he had set out to do so many years before, and all this alongside hundreds of other projects. The first of the quotes below from a speech given in church tells us a great deal about the man.

Quotes:

"I love humanity, which has been a constant delight to me during all my seventy-seven years of life; and I love flowers, trees, animals, and all the works of Nature as they pass before us in time and space. What a joy life is when you have made a close working partnership with Nature, helping her to produce for the benefit of mankind new forms, colors, and perfumes in flowers which were never known before; fruits in form, size, and flavor never before seen on this globe; and grains of enormously increased productiveness, whose fat kernels are filled with more and better nourishment, a veritable storehouse of perfect food--new food for all the world's untold millions for all time to come."

"Flowers always make people better, happier and more helpful; they are sunshine, food and medicine to the soul."

46. Edward W. Bok

Born 9th October 1863 – Died 9th January 1930 Like Arthur Brisbane, Edward Andrew Bok was one of the most influential writers of his day. Again in common with Brisbane, Bok authored a number of books but is primarily remembered for his work in popular printed media, in the case of Bok primarily the magazine Ladies Home Journal.

Born in Den Helder in the Netherlands his family emigrated, taking him to the United States and settling in Brooklyn when the lad was six years old. He attended a public school, which means a state school, not the upper class paid education that is referred to by the term Public School in Great Britain. Bok's parents were so impoverished that at the age of twelve he left education and took a job with the Western Union Telegraph Company as an office boy. However, in his own time he wrote biographies of notable Americans and sold them for $10 a piece. It's very difficult now to calculate accurately the value of that in today's money as there are different possible criteria. Using consumer pricing as a measure then in 2009 that $10 would represent $200, however if relative earnings are compared over the same time lapse then it would be considerably more than $200. However one views it the young Bok was already an entrepreneur.

In 1882 he went to work for a publishing company called Henry Holt & Co. His work there was as a stenographer, which is to say transcribing the spoken word into shorthand for record keeping rather than dictation, although sound recording was in its infancy (see Hill's Heroes Thomas Edison and Alexander Bell). In 1884 he moved to the more prominent publishers Charles Scribner & Sons where he fulfilled a number of roles but ultimately became Advertising Manager. He also edited a church based magazine called the Brooklyn Magazine and in 1886 started Bok Syndicate Press which involved him in newspaper publishing for a while.

The opportunity which really made Bok came in 1889 when publishing magnate Cyrus H.K. Curtis invited Bok to replace his wife Louise, who wanted to take a less active role in the business, as editor of Ladies Home Journal. Bok would edit this publication for the next thirty years. Using this magazine he influenced greatly the American way of life and in many ways the British too since American ideas tend to cross the pond! Boks ideals were common sense, hard work, service to others and self improvement; ideals which he believed led to success. He tried to influence and improve the lives of middle class Americans, he advocated sex education for children, affordable housing, conservation through his 'Beautiful America' campaign and he attacked patented medicines refusing advertising for them in the magazine.

Circulation figures rose dramatically under Bok's stewardship, the magazine becoming the first in America and probably therefore in the world to reach one million readers, a milestone reached in 1903. However, by 1893 Bok was already Vice President of the Curtis Publishing Company and in 1896 married Mary Louise Curtis, daughter of Cyrus and Louise. Bok retired in 1919 to write and indulge his passion for philanthropy. His autobiography 'The Americanisation Of Edward Bok' won both the gold medal of the Academy of Political and Social Science and the Pulitzer Prize. Bok's wife shared his passion for philanthropy and supported young musicians in particular, creating the Curtis Institute of Music dedicated to her father. Bok himself established a number of public endowments and created the Bok Tower and Gardens as a sanctuary for Americans which was inaugurated by President Calvin Coolidge and is an American National Monument to this day.

By the time of his death in 1930 Bok had given away over $2 million to charitable causes including a $100,000 American Peace Award. Bok believed the U.S. government was not doing enough to support world peace and his award was for 'the best practical plan by which the U.S. may cooperate with other nations for the achievement and preservation of world peace'. The money was to be paid in two instalments half to be paid when the best plan was selected and the second half when the U.S. Senate accepted it. There were thousands of entries and the award was given to Dr Charles Herbert Levermore in February 1924 on the basis that the U.S. should adhere to the Permanent Court of International Justice and extend it's cooperation with the League of Nations.

Of course the League failed but it is interesting to see that a number of Hill's Heroes worked for world peace, notably Bok, Ford and Carnegie. Bok's influence on our lives today is underlined by our adoption of the term 'living room', where previously families had a parlour or a drawing room reserved for 'best', that is for visitors or special occasions, Bok thought such rooms should be used as evidenced by the quote below. Not only was Bok a hero of Hill's but he also features in another iconic book 'How To Win Friends And Influence People' by Dale Carnegie.

Quote:

We have what is called a 'drawing room'. Just whom or what it 'draws' I have never been able to see unless it draws attention to too much money and no taste..."

47. Frank A. Munsey

Born August 21st 1854 in Mercer Maine – Died December 22nd 1925. Frank Andrew Mercer was another of Hill's Heroes who might be described as a publishing baron, in this case quite a controversial though innovative and interesting one. Munsey may be considered the father of pulp fiction but there is much more to his story than that.

The son of hard working parents he was described as a sober and industrious boy. His first venture was to run a general store, at which he failed, before taking a job, in common with a number of Hill's Heroes, as a telegraph operator for the Western Union Telegraph Company where he was a success and quickly rose to be manager of the Augusta office. However, he left in 1882 lured to New York, inspired by we know not what, although Augusta had a considerable publishing sector that he would have had contact with through Western Union news wires, with ambitions to become a publisher. He left with the rights to a handful of stories he had purchased.

Munsey's own story is one of persistence, overcoming failure and opposition and learning from mistakes. He may have failed as a store keeper but one day he would own a whole chain of them. In the early days he had to borrow money and deal with the disappointment of a financial backer pulling out. He worked for a publishing company that went into receivership owing him his wages, but this problem he turned into an opportunity, he took legal action to recover his wages and ultimately took over the failed company and after a struggle made it pay. Now he was on his way.

His first publication was called Golden Argosy, an adventure magazine aimed at boys. It became simply The Argosy and was now targeted at an older audience Munsey having realised that kids had little spending power in his day and that advertisers accordingly were not interested. Later still this publication became the monthly Argosy Magazine but alone it would not fulfil Munsey's goals.

In 1889 Munsey's magazine is created which he described as being of the people, for the people, it was upbeat, entertaining and with human interest. It soon sold forty thousand copies a week and its strategy is apparent in many of the magazines we see today. Munsey always adapted and innovated, in 1891 the magazine became monthly, in 1892 it included an entire novel in each edition and in 1893 the price dropped to ten cents. Munsey was a pioneer in that he realised that advertising effectiveness depended upon numbers and he linked his advertising rates to circulation which rose dramatically with the lower cover price.

This move scared many in the industry and he lost his distribution privileges with American News Co., undeterred Munsey set up his own distribution and after a relatively short battle broke the monopoly. This combined with high speed presses and low cost pulp paper led to circulation of half a million by 1895 and seven hundred thousand by 1897. Munsey produced a range of magazines aimed at specific audiences such as railroad men, sailors, mechanics, and children once more. While they made money he kept them, when interest waned he killed them off, a policy he then applied to newspapers.

He used his profits from the magazines to invest in a large portfolio of newspapers some lost money, others made money but always he consolidated and killed off the weak. This policy made him enemies, not least amongst journalists but he believed weak publications deserved to die. As an example of his spending power a single takeover of the New York Herald, Paris Herald and New York Evening Telegram cost him four million dollars in 1920.

Munsey was very active politically, being one of the main supporters of Hill's Hero Theodore Roosevelt in his battle with, ironically, another of Hill's Heroes William Howard Taft and unlike Bok he was opposed to The League Of Nations. He wrote a number of books, never married and was possibly worth forty million dollars on death, perhaps as much as half a billion dollars in today's money. He bequeathed money to extended family, managers within his businesses and to a lady who in his youth declined a proposal of marriage believing he would never be a success. This annuity to Annie Downs and his investing in a chain of stores having failed as a store keeper possibly gives us an insight into the character of the man. He also left money to Bowdoin College, two hospitals and a large bequest to the Metropolitan Museum Of Art. Munsey Park, New York was founded on land he once owned.

Quote:

"With me there has never been anything very terrible about changing a publication as often as conditions warranted, and in making the change as radical as I pleased."

48. Elbert H. Gary

Born October 8th 1846 – Died August 15th 1927. Napoleon Hill makes much of Charles M. Schwab's billion dollar deal and of course tells us a great deal about Andrew Carnegie who naturally figures strongly in Think And Grow Rich, being the man who inspired Hill's own mission in life. When we examine the lives of Hill's Heroes in greater detail we see something of a boom and bust character in Schwab but a life of constant achievement in that of Elbert H. Gary.

Born on a farm near Wheaton, Illinois to devout Methodist parents it's quite incredible just how much Gary fitted into one lifetime. Mayor, President of the Chicago Bar Association, Bank Founder, lawyer and judge, property investor, philanthropist and Church builder as well as Sunday School teacher and choir member for twenty years. However he is best remembered as Chairman of U.S. Steel the first billion dollar corporation in American history.

Having graduated top of his class at the Union College of Law in 1868 (later the Northwestern University School of Law) Gary started a law practice with offices in Chicago and Wheaton. He would primarily practice law for the next twenty five years, alongside his church commitments, yet he still found time to found the Gary-Wheaton Bank with his Uncle

Jesse Wheaton, a business which survived under that name until a merger with Bank One Corporation in the 1990s. He invested in building and property, served two terms as a Du Page County judge from 1884 and was elected the first Mayor of Wheaton when it officially became a City in 1890, it had only the status of village until that time! He spurned opportunities for higher office and built a considerable reputation as a corporate lawyer especially after the Chicago Fire.

This reputation brought John Gates, someone he had grown up with but not always got along with to his door when he needed advice concerning the merger of several barbed wire businesses. Although the two men had not been friends Gates trusted Gary, who duly did a good job for him. However, the experience fired Gary's own interest in the business and in 1898 at the age of fifty two and some twenty seven years after first going into law professionally he became President of Federal Steel Corporation in Chicago. It was in this capacity that he became a member, with Gates of the group of men who put together U.S. Steel. So impressed by Gary's skills at this juncture was J.P. Morgan that he told Gary he could name his own board of directors and his own salary but he had to be President and Chairman of the Board of the new venture. Gary duly became just that, serving until his death at age eighty two. On leaving Wheaton for a life in New York, Gary built the old town a large new church and left an endowment for its upkeep.

The town of Gary Indiana was laid out by the company in 1906 and named after its famous president; by 1908, after expenditure of $42 million it was the world's largest integrated steel making complex and worker's town. Though the men differed politically Gary was a friend of Hill's Hero and trust busting President Theodore Roosevelt and felt that Roosevelt's description of him as head of the 'Steel Trust' was a compliment. Roosevelt's relationship with other men he viewed as heads of trusts was not so cordial.

Gary promoted profit sharing, higher wages, better working conditions and pensions but working hours remained long and he was strongly opposed to unions. In 1909 he founded the American Iron And Steel Institute to stabilise prices. An antitrust suit brought against the company and Gary's policies failed in the Supreme Court in 1919 the year of the steel strike. Gary felt that "we (the company) are not obliged to contract with unions if we do not choose to do so". He declined to arbitrate and broke the strike. As was customary at the time he was known as Judge Gary from his appointment until his death. He had purchased a farm in New York State to escape from the pressures and doubtless to remind him of his boyhood, but he was still at the helm of U.S. Steel, as he had been for twenty six years, when he passed away.

49. Dr. Alexander Graham Bell

Born March 3rd 1847 – Died August 2nd 1922 Dr Alexander Graham Bell has arguably affected our lives today more than any other of Hill's Heroes whilst his humanity and character are also of great interest. Bell's father was a teacher of the deaf and his mother a musician and painter gradually lost her hearing as Bell grew up. Bell's early education was in the home, in Edinburgh, Scotland, where he taught himself to play the piano, inspired to do so by his mother and where he innovated ways of communicating better with his beloved mother as her hearing deteriorated to profound deafness.

Bell's father was a pioneer of what we today call lip reading and which he called visible speech, he taught the deaf how the lips tongue and throat work to produce sound and helped those deaf from birth to speak. Bell himself became proficient and had a lifelong interest in the subject, as well as acoustics generally and sound transmission also as a result. This work undoubtedly helped him to develop what the modern world considers his greatest invention, the telephone.

Sadly much controversy and many court cases surrounded this invention and the application for the patent. It seems likely that Bell's competitors drew as much on his work as he may, or may not have done on theirs. Bell's depth of understanding of sound dates back to his childhood and this should support his claim, further to that his ongoing work with the telephone and sound transmission has had a deep impact on modern life and is key to much we now take for granted as you will see shortly.

Bell did attend Edinburgh Royal High School briefly but was not inspired by the classics, having a greater interest in science. At the age of eleven he was given the middle name Graham, something he requested and done out of respect for a student of his father's. At age twelve he developed a de-husking machine for a neighbour who ran a flour mill, while he and his brother Melville fashioned a model head that could be made to emit human sounding speech. However, despite his inventiveness and enquiring mind he was considered a poor pupil at school and left at the age of fourteen. He then spent a year then with his grandfather in London, the old man taught him much and gave him access to a considerable library which Bell availed himself of keenly.

Returning to Scotland, at sixteen he enrolled at Weston House Academy to both teach and study whilst the following year he briefly attended Edinburgh University with brother Melville. Shortly after, in 1865 the family moved to London. Melville left home married and started his own elocution business. Whilst Bell returned to Weston House as a teacher, continuing his own experiments with electricity and telegraphy in his spare time.

In 1867 younger brother Edward contracted tuberculosis from which he would not recover. Bell became ill for a while but seemed to recover and took a position at Somerset College, Bath. When his younger brother died Bell returned home to help his father in teaching the deaf something he was very successful at. In 1870 the promising life of his brother Melville was tragically cut short by complications, again from tuberculosis and Bell himself was not in perfect health. The family took the decision to expedite a long held ambition to emigrate to Canada, Bell's father once having recuperated from illness there.

Settled on a farm near Brantford, Ontario Bell continued working with his father, conducting his own experiments and additionally found time to learn the Mohawk language from local Indians for whom he also created a written form, the language having hitherto been verbal only. His health recovered. Bell's father was invited to speak about his visible speech programme in the USA but nominated his son who spent six months in the USA before returning to Canada. However this experience led to Bell setting up his own school in Boston where he taught among others Hill's Hero Helen Keller and his own future wife Mabel Hubbard ten years his junior and deaf as a result of scarlet fever at age four which had nearly killed her.

Bell, as always continued his own experiments and scientific probings which would lead him to invent the telephone, although his health suffered once more as a result of the hours he spent working and he was forced to cut back on his teaching. With financial backing from the families of two of his pupils including the father of his future wife he was able to employ an assistant, an electrical engineer named Thomas Watson. He had already invented a harmonic system for transmitting multiple telegraph messages down a single wire utilising different frequencies, something Western Union had contracted Elisha Gray, (one of the two main protagonists in claiming prior invention of the telephone) and Hill's Hero Edison to look into. This invention influenced and encouraged Bell's backers who would become millionaires from their association with him.

Bell had designed a telephone and worked out the principles, when on February 14th 1876 he sent a lawyer to the patent office to file a patent, he himself remaining in Boston. Interestingly he had delayed sending in the application in order to first obtain a patent in Britain, the patent office there not accepting applications where an invention had already been patented in another country. Had he disregarded this then subsequent controversy may have been avoided. Bell's lawyer is supposed to have beaten Elisha Gray to the door of the U.S. office by one hour although Elisha Gray would later dispute this in court.

Nonetheless the U.S. patent was awarded to Bell on March 7th 1876. It was three days later that Bell famously spoke by telephone to Watson in the next room, saying "Mr Watson, come here I want you". It is claimed he did so having obtained details about Gray's patent application and that he used a liquid transmitter to do so. This may well be the case, however, he never used a liquid transmitter before obtaining his own patent, nor did he use one later and certainly not commercially, developing instead his own electromagnetic telephone.

There may have been some skulduggery and we may never know the full details, or whether Bell was involved, or whether the lawyer despatched to the patent office took advantage of the self confessed alcoholic inspector, maybe on his own initiative, much is now speculation. Certainly the Bell company were also victims themselves, being beaten to the patent in Germany by the Siemens company who's initial telephone was suspiciously similar to Bell's, Siemens made millions from it.

The U.S. patent was however awarded to Bell and was subsequently offered to the Western Union Telegraph Company for $100,000. The president of that company thought the price too high for what he considered a toy. Later he would confide to friends that it would have been a bargain at $25 million! Bell and his associates started the Bell Telephone company in 1877 and transformed the world. Bell himself demonstrated the device to Queen Victoria who immediately wanted all her castles connected by wire.

In that same year Bell married Mabel Hubbard, embarked on a year long honeymoon around Europe with her and gave her as a wedding present 1,487 of his 1,497 shares in the Bell Telephone company. By 1917 virtually the entire United States had a telephone service, but Bell had long since turned his attentions to other scientific and engineering achievements. Although he was distracted by numerous and protracted court cases concerning his invention and his patent. Elisha Gray's case was eventually dismissed by the Supreme Court but there were many other cases.

An Italian inventor Antonio Meucci claimed to have invented the telephone as early 1834, if so what did he do with it? This claim was rejected at the time due to lack of material evidence whilst the claims of Amos Dolbear and Elisha Gray were weakened by prior admissions in correspondence with Bell that they had drawn on his work. While his own case was strengthened by his lifelong demonstrable interest and work with acoustics and sound transmission.

The Bell company won all it's court battles but the strain imposed on Bell himself led to his resignation from the company. He had taken U.S. citizenship and declined dual nationality, being devoted to his adopted country yet in 2002 the U.S. House of representatives, convinced by a member of that august body, one of Italian ancestry, finally stripped him symbolically of his patent in favour of Meucci, whilst the Canadian Government passed a bill confirming Bell as the inventor of the telephone. One could hope that politicians would find more useful outlets for their time, and energy and our resources.

The controversy is a great shame for it distracts us from Bell's many achievements. Admirably, he himself considered the telephone an intrusive device that distracted him from his work and he refused to have one in his study. Numerous honours were heaped upon him in his lifetime and since. Most notably the Volta Prize of France 50,000 French Franks, around U.S.$10,000 at the time enabled Bell, in 1881, to set up the Volta research facility in Washington DC with his cousin Chichester Bell and Charles Sumner Tainter, amongst other things they here made Hill's Hero Edison's phonograph commercially viable.

Around 1886 he set up another research facility in Nova Scotia for bright young scientists and engineers dividing his time between that community in Canada and his American projects. In his lifetime he was awarded eighteen patents, twelve of these with collaborators. When President Garfield was shot by an assassin he immediately invented a metal detector to help surgeons locate the bullet. the sceptical surgeons refused to move the President to a bed without a metal frame and springs and Bell was unable to precisely locate the bullet, but archaeologists, treasure hunters and those who have had to detect land mines may be more grateful. When Bell's newborn son tragically died of respiratory illness he invented the forerunner of the iron lung which helped numerous polio victims and itself is the precursor of modern life support systems.

Together with Charles Sumner Tainter he invented a way of transmitting sound using light, the principles have helped us develop fibre optics and impact our technological lives today. He had a visionary interest in alternative fuels, and green issues such as composting toilets, he envisaged, although did not invent, the solar panel, he developed desalination equipment so we could get fresh water from sea water and looked at ways of obtaining water from the atmosphere. He even invented a device to locate icebergs at sea.

At the age of sixty, in 1891, he became interested in aircraft and experimented with tetrahedral kites; his wife commenting on his age encouraged him to find younger collaborators, so with Glenn Curtiss, William 'Casey' Baldwin, Thomas Selfridge and J.A.D. Mc Murdy he formed the Aerial Experiment Association in 1907. This was just four years after the Wright Brothers flew at Kitty Hawk and within two years they had built four aircraft, the most famous and successful being the Silver Dart which made the first successful powered flight in Canada February 23rd 1909. Curtiss went on to found the famous aircraft company named after him, truly these men were pioneers.

Like Elbert H. Gary above Bell worked to the very end, he was a founding member of The National Geographic Society and its president for several years, for the last ten years of his life he devoted himself largely to the development of the Hydrofoil and created a speed record on water of over seventy miles per hour which stood for many years. This lifelong enquiry into the mysteries of the world and the drive of the inventor are underlined by the quotes below.

On August 2nd 1922 he passed away in Nova Scotia where he had become a much admired villager in the local community. Mabel whispered to him "Don't leave me." Too weak to speak he traced the sign for no and expired. His coffin was made by his staff from local pine and lined with the red silk used for his kites, at the close of his funeral every telephone in North America was briefly silenced as a mark of respect.

Quotes:

"There cannot be mental atrophy in any person who continues to observe, to remember what he observes, and to seek answers for his unceasing hows and whys about things."

"The most successful men in the end are those whose success is the result of steady accretion."

50. John H. Patterson

Born December 13th 1844 – Died May 7th 1922 John H. Patterson founded one of the great manufacturing companies of his age NCR or National Cash Register Inc. to give it its full title. He has been described as the worst CEO (Chief Executive Officer) in history as amongst other things he had a habit of hiring and firing people, it is said to break them. Most famously he hired and then fired Thomas Watson who went on to create IBM. He was accused of being what we today might call a control freak and more worryingly was accused of hiring thugs to ensure storekeepers did not buy rival products. He was jointly tried and convicted with others under Anti-Trust laws and sentenced to a year in jail, overturned on appeal, so just why is he one of Hill's Heroes, especially given the first of the two quotes by Napoleon Hill reproduced near the beginning of this book, the one concerning honesty.

To understand John Henry Patterson it's necessary to look at his life overall. He was born of tough revolutionary stock. His grandfather fought under Washington and founded Lexington, and lived with the family on the farm where Patterson was raised. Before school Patterson would have to cut his grandfather's fire wood and build his fire, then put the calves out. After school he would have to do more farm work and then study after supper.

After graduating from Dartmouth College in 1867, his previous education at Miami University having been interrupted by the civil war in which he served the Union for one hundred days as a volunteer, life remained hard. He worked on the farm for a while then briefly taught school and then collected tolls on the canal. This last job was twenty four hours seven days a week and the pay was poor, as a sideline he sold coal and expanded this business until he could leave the canal job completely.

The coal business, in which his brother helped him expanded, Patterson instinctively understood the need for customer satisfaction at minimum he sold quality coal and went out of his way to demonstrate honesty by introducing receipts for monies paid and goods delivered, then he went the extra mile by visiting customers at home to teach them how to build and light a good fire. He encouraged the building of a new, more direct railroad and advertised widely and effectively. The coal business boomed, but it alongside it Patterson was running a store where dishonest clerks were possibly swindling as much as $18,000 dollars per annum. Various sources offer conflicting information, but it is possible the store should have made as much as $12,000 dollars a year in profit and actually lost $3,000 to $6,000.

Patterson purchased two more or less prototype cash registers called Riddy's Incorruptible Cashiers. Realising the potential was vast not just for the store he was trying to run, but right across America and around the world he bought the company with help from his brother and two smaller stockholders who he would later buy out. Of the 300 initial shares he held two hundred and twenty seven his brother only one. Clearly he thought big, another man might just have sorted the store out and carried on.

Having acquired the company he set about manufacturing and doing so in a way that involved efficient practices and precision work. The company soon expanded but Patterson's pioneering work didn't stop there. In an age of sweat shops, he built a factory with floor to ceiling glass and windows that opened to let fresh air in. He provided good food for his employees at cost price and rest periods too. He created America's first sales school in the grounds of his factory and his methods influenced American business for a generation. Indeed he may justifiably be regarded as the father of professional selling. It is said that between 1910 and 1930 one sixth of all U.S. executives were former NCR men. Every office in his service division displayed on its wall the slogan 'We Cannot Afford Even One Dissatisfied Customer' and later he would lecture widely on the business practices that made NCR so successful.

He responded to child vandalism by providing a place for the local children to go and be taught modelling, carving, drawing and gardening, girls were taught sewing, embroidery and cooking. Today we may see this as stereotyping, but back then to respond to vandalism in such a creative and positive way was revolutionary and we cannot blame Patterson for being a product of his age in some ways. His efforts in this area led to the creation of The Children's Garden Movement of America and he beautified his local community too offering prizes for the best kept lawns and other initiatives.

His brother had been a considerable support to Patterson in the business, but he died suddenly in 1901. Patterson took more upon himself and travelled far and wide setting up the international business. This workload led to a breakdown in 1904 from which he recovered, however it made him more obsessed with healthy living and led to his trying to enforce healthy ideals on his workers. Possibly this is where some of the accusations against him stem from.

His finest hour came in 1913 with the event of the Great Dayton Flood, cometh the hour, cometh the man. He turned his employees over to building flat bottomed boats, nearly three hundred were built in a great hurry and Patterson organised rescue teams to save hundreds of people trapped on roofs and in upper stories. He turned his factory into a sanctuary for the refugees and provided food and medical care as well as shelter. When the flood waters receded he got together the local civic leaders at a meeting in his school and organised future flood defences to which he donated a great deal personally.

When the USA entered World War One he put his factory at the disposal of the government and was entrusted with producing precision parts in a rush, something his workforce were well up to. To escape the stresses of the business he created a summer estate on Beaver Lake so he could enjoy the Adirondack Mountains and take care of his health. He planned a centre for aviation research, another interest of several of Hill's Heroes, but died before it could be realised. After the war he again travelled widely in Europe this time to learn and to do good. It's noticeable how many of Hill's Heroes had an interest in World Peace including Henry Ford, Andrew Carnegie and others. When we look at the second quote in the section on Napoleon Hill we can see that Patterson was truly fitted to be one of his Heroes; Patterson's last trip abroad was to The Association Of Nations For World Peace.

Patterson's numerous social programmes meant that he left no huge monetary fortune, in common with Carnegie he believed that to die rich was an error. He did leave his company to his son and when he took it public in 1925 $55 million of stock was offered to the public, the largest U.S. flotation up to that time.

Quotes:

"An executive is a person who always decides sometimes he decides correctly, but he always decides."

"To survive, men and business and corporations must serve."

"To succeed in business it is necessary to make others see things as you see them."

"Before you try to convince anyone else, be sure you are convinced, and if you cannot convince yourself, drop the subject."

CPSIA information can be obtained at www.ICGtesting.com
Printed in the USA
LVOW072015161012

303111LV00023B/28/P